ASTROLOGY
FOR **TODAY**

ASTROLOGY
FOR TODAY

Joanna Watters

CARROLL & BROWN PUBLISHERS LIMITED

CONTENTS

First published in 2003 in the United Kingdom by
Carroll & Brown Publishers Limited
20 Lonsdale Road, London, NW6 6RD

Managing Editor Michelle Bernard
Designer Jim Cheatle

A CIP catalogue record for this book is available
from the British Library

ISBN 1 903258 69 3

10987654321

Reproduced by RALI S.A., Spain
Printed and bound in Spain by Bookprint

INTRODUCTION

If you have opened this book you will be somewhere on the continuum of curious to fascinated with regard to astrology. The subject may be completely new to you and you could be wondering if it is worth finding out more. You may already be an avid student, hungry for more information.

It may be that you are drowning in information about astrology and have now reached that all too familiar point of confusion where, if you don't get to grips with this subject soon, you will be tempted to give up. Or you may already be a fully fledged astrologer in your own right with your own clients, seeking new ideas and fresh input. No matter how far along the path you may be, this is a book for people who have let astrology into their lives.

However, this book is also for astrology's critics. Skepticism can be a very healthy and positive thing, as long as it is used to question and investigate rather than to ridicule. I freely and happily admit that, at the beginning of my own foray into astrology, I too was deeply skeptical. I had been intrigued by the subject for as long as I could remember, but my first experience as a client, nearly 20 years ago, left me deeply disappointed as I came away none the wiser. Rather than finding answers, I ended up with even more questions and the feeling that, surely, there must be more to astrology than that. My only option then was to find out for myself, which I promptly did with the Company of Astrologers in London.

I remember vividly, especially during the first 12 months, that voracious hunger for knowledge—the hours and hours spent reading, studying, and experimenting; the many moments of frustration when nothing seemed to fit or make sense; and then the satisfying turning points when the light bulb would flash and details would drop into place. From my own subsequent experience as a tutor I can assure you that I was not unusual in this respect. Even with the best tuition and all the will and enthusiasm in the world, many students maintain a healthy doubt as they persist in their studies, waiting for their own particular moment of "proof."

This belies the scorn so often voiced by undeniably intelligent people, that those who turn to astrology must be sadly gullible and impressionable, or so insecure that they simply want astrology to be true. There is a widespread assumption that people embrace astrology unquestioningly and that their conviction is rooted solely in their need for a comforting crutch. I have only to think about my colleagues, the students I have taught, and my clients to know that this is certainly not the case. In fact, nothing could be further from the truth. Never have I encountered such discerning, interesting people than within the astrological community.

MYSTICAL NONSENSE?

It is quite remarkable how astrology can be so easily dumped on some kind of mystical scrapheap by those who are normally inquiring, probing, and articulate. These same people would almost certainly give any other subject their deepest thought and consideration. Yet mention astrology and frequently you will hear dismissive comments such as, "it's all a load of nonsense." Eminent scientist, Richard Dawkins, author of *The Selfish Gene*, is the ultimate example. He has raged against the subject so fiercely that he has even talked of suing astrologers. Something has gone sadly wrong when a subject can provoke such a deep and hostile divide.

So what is the debate really about? It appears that it is not simply a question of someone being right and someone being wrong. If that were the case then an argument for either side could be either successfully upheld or dismantled, and that would be the end of the controversy. But astrology has been around since the 5th century BC and has so far proved itself indestructible.

Similarly, the supremacy of the scientific world view in Western culture shows no sign of weakening either. So it is time to look through the other end of the telescope. Rather than a pointless attempt to dismantle a conflicting point of view it is far more effective to look at the enduring misconceptions that have created the conflict in the first place.

DYNAMIC SYMBOLISM

Firstly, astrologers do not "believe in" their subject. It is not a belief system or a faith, terms that generally suggest some level of blindness. Astrologers know their craft in the way that other craftspeople know theirs, through learning, practice, and the honing of skills. Secondly, you do not have to be a witch or clairvoyant to be an astrologer. Some astrologers may possess psychic abilities and these may be an

"In some shape or form, astrology appears in virtually every culture of the world.... It is older than science and shows no signs of going away."

Maggie Hyde and Geoffrey Cornelius

advantage, but they are not essential, because astrology is not just about "seeing" the future but about discovering meaning and purpose.

The conception of astrology as dynamic symbolism rather than as a causal, determining, or fatalistic influence is crucial to the thesis of this book. This is not to suggest that there is nothing magical about astrology but that it is simply in astrology's best interests to refute the idea of a vital link between horoscopy—astrological craft—and second sight.

Mars is a symbol for war and action.

Of course, this generally isn't in the commercial interest, and the predictive face of astrology is the only one that thrives in the media. In this respect it is easy to see how astrology can give out the wrong message and how, to add insult to injury, it then appears to claim an alignment with science. This is because a horoscope originates from a scientific premise, in that the astrologer starts with specific and objective data that roots a horoscope firmly in time and place. But this is where astrology and astronomy divide, and where the symbolism versus science argument begins. For astronomers, Mars, for example, is the red planet between the Earth and Jupiter, but for astrologers, Mars is the symbol for such things as war, anger, men, passion, and action. To be an astrologer is to be, first and foremost, a symbolist. Whatever we observe about any astrological feature must always be translated symbolically, as you will find in the following pages, and failure to grasp this point is the biggest single contributory factor in common misconceptions.

Yet astrology does not always play by the rules that we would like to impose because meaning can, and frequently does, manifest itself in non-scientific ways. This is the basis of the eternal accusation that astrologers are imprecise and vague, that they will resort to generalization so that, with a little twisting, what they say could fit anyone. This is the most common criticism leveled at Sun sign columns and is, in my opinion, justified. In modern times, astrology has survived largely thanks to this format, but, at the same time, has undermined itself by donning the symbolic straitjacket of fortune-telling.

FLUID INTERPRETATION

Horoscopy is a world away from Sun sign columns but is tarred with the same brush. It is only when we perceive astrology as non-causal—that the planets themselves don't make us do or be anything, they are not the cause of our behavior, personality, or life events—that it can stand on its own two feet. It is only human assignation of symbolic meaning that makes astrology work. When you add the second vital ingredient of recognizing astrology as a symbolic language, the nature and point of the craft starts to make sense, because symbolism, by its nature, cannot be categorized beyond a certain point. At an objective, mathematical level the horoscope is just a piece of paper covered in hieroglyphics, but at a subjective level it becomes the symbolic context for an individual and his or her life. The chart does not mean anything until it is addressed by both astrologer and client together, which is why written or computerized charts don't work and are never more than a shot in the dark. Preconceived ideas and interpretations can toll the death knell for the astrologer's understanding, and for this reason you will not find lists of keywords for every combination of planet, sign, or aspect in this book. You will find, I hope, a fluid and non-categorizing approach to astrological symbolism that is aimed at keeping your interpretations fresh, sharp, and, more importantly, real.

The main premise of this book is not to prove astrology but to demonstrate it, at work and at play. To this end I have included the basic mathematics and working examples for both natal chart calculation and progressions—the technique of moving a chart on year by year. It is tempting for the newcomer to fall back on software to do the figures but, invariably, this is a short cut to nowhere because it often leads to technical sloppiness. At the outset there is no substitute for pen, paper, and calculator, because being able to understand how a chart works at a physical, objective level is directly related to our understanding of a chart at a subjective and symbolic level. The tighter our craft discipline, the more likely it is that we will encounter powerful, rich, and lively symbolism. In other words, technical accuracy is the springboard to meaningful interpretation and one cannot exist without the other.

At an interpretative level I have attempted throughout the book to bring astrology to life either by using celebrity examples or by recounting anecdotes and case histories from my own practice. Within these stories runs the thread of astrological consulting, how the astrologer must always acknowledge the responsibility of touching on other people's lives, and how to translate astrological language in a way that makes a horoscope both accessible and intelligible.

For those readers who are just discovering astrology, I hope the material presented in this book will provide enough basic information and guidelines to provoke your continued interest. For readers who are further down the road, I hope this book will give you plenty to get your teeth into and that it may revive flagging energies and enthusiasm. Although I have tried to allow space for the philosophy, meaning, and practice of astrology, this work is not specifically aimed at the astrological intellectual. It is aimed at bridging the gap between information and meaning for the ordinary astrologer in modern times, people such as myself, and is presented to you with Sagittarian straightforwardness. May your knowledge expand and all of your astrological arrows hit the mark.

Astrology divides the circle of the heavens into 12 segments, corresponding to the 12 signs of the zodiac, and your astrological sign is determined by the position of the Sun on your date of birth. Each of the 12 signs symbolizes certain qualities and characteristics that can be expressed in a multitude of ways. Understanding the unique nature of each sign is the first rung on the ladder of chart interpretation.

SUN SIGNS

INTRODUCING THE SIGNS

Astrology begins with Sun signs. Even if you have never opened a book on the subject you will know your Sun sign, just as you know your name and your age. Your Sun sign is a factor of your personal identity, something that you have never consciously learned but have always known. You may know some characteristics of your sign, but probably little more.

The unflagging popularity of Sun sign columns has kept astrology in our cultural consciousness for the last 70 years, and astrology's survival owes much to this format. Unfortunately, this survival is a double-edged sword as media-orientated astrology is the basis of common misconceptions and often ridicule.

Learning about Sun signs is the first step on the astrological voyage of discovery, and in this chapter you will find a full description of each sign. However, it is important to remember that talking about a sign in isolation can be very different from seeing it in context, as an integral part of a complete horoscope. The full range of meaning starts to come home when we marry up signs with planets and all the other factors in a working horoscope. But a sound grasp of Sun sign symbolism is the core of astrological knowledge, from which all other factors evolve and make sense.

A trap with Sun sign astrology is that it can lead to generalization. In the following pages I have tried to illustrate the typical characteristics of each sign, while at the same time drawing attention to the wider range of meaning inherent in the signs. Rather than attributing universal characteristics to one sign, it can be much more enlightening to think how each sign's symbolism is particular to itself.

For instance, many people associate Gemini, the sign of the twins, with a split personality, the Jekyll and Hyde of the zodiac, and it is true that Gemini is a changeable sign. However, it is also true that we all have our light side and dark side, whether we have Gemini in our chart or not. The real clue to Gemini lies in its youthfulness and duality that operate at different levels. It is these characteristics that are the essence of this sign.

As you learn more about astrology, you will build an astrological vocabulary. The first lesson of this new language is the shorthand—the glyphs, or symbols, that astrologers use for the signs and planets.

BORN ON THE CUSP

If you are born on a day when the Sun moves from one sign to another this is called being born on the cusp. This is not to be confused with "house cusps," which are covered in chapter three, and are the lines that divide one house (one of the 12 segments of a chart) from the next.

GLYPHS FOR SUN SIGNS

ARIES: *the Ram. This glyph symbolizes the pointed face and horns of the ram.*

TAURUS: *the Bull. This glyph symbolizes the round face and horned head of the bull.*

GEMINI: *the Twins. The two vertical and horizontal lines symbolize the duality of the twins.*

CANCER: *the Crab. This glyph speaks of fertility, symbolizing sperm or the roundness of breasts.*

LEO: *the Lion. This glyph symbolizes the lion's face and the flourish of the mane.*

VIRGO: *the Maiden or Virgin. The letter "M" combined with the crossed legs of the virgin.*

LIBRA: *the Scales. Symbolizes the principle of symmetry and balance.*

SCORPIO: *the Scorpion. The letter "M," with the upward-pointing sting of the scorpion's tail.*

SAGITTARIUS: *the Centaur or Archer. Symbolizes the bow and arrow slanting upward and to the future.*

CAPRICORN: *the Mountain Goat. Symbolizes the bony face and curling horns of the goat.*

AQUARIUS: *The Water Bearer. Pointed waves symbolizing air waves rather than the sea.*

PISCES: *the Fishes. Symbolizes the two fish swimming in opposite directions.*

It is a common misconception that being born as the Sun is changing signs makes you a combination of two signs, but the truth is that you are either one or the other, never both. So how do you find out if you were is born at the very end of one sign or at the very beginning of the next?

There are 30 degrees in each sign and the Sun moves at a rate of just under or over 1 degree a day. But the 12 signs of the zodiac do not correspond to the 12 months of the year, as each sign starts at around the 21st of the month. Also, every year the Sun moves into a sign at different times—even a different day—so you will need to check the ephemerides for accurate information.

WHAT ARE EPHEMERIDES?

The word ephemerides is derived from the word "ephemeral," meaning daily. Ephemerides are the tables that list the daily motions of the planets—the signs they are in and how fast they are moving. Always buy an ephemerides that includes an aspectarian—a section that lists the aspects of the day. This is indispensable when working with progressions, (see chapter six) but it also gives the dates and times of ingresses—when a planet changes sign. (For more detailed information on ephemerides, see chapter three.)

The diagram on page 15 shows the elements and modes on the horoscopic wheel—every fourth sign sharing the same element, every third sign sharing the same mode (+ = a masculine sign, and – = feminine.) The more quickly you can learn the elements and modes, the faster your

The ephemeris table (the following values are transcribed as printed in the dense aspectarian grid):

22	21 23	02 N 22	1 05:35 ☽ ♂ ♂	6 00:35 ⊙ ♀ ☽	19:39 ☽ △ ♂	14:53 ☽ ⚻ ♄	21:06 ☽ △ ♂	23 01:45 ☽ ⚹ ♂	12:55 ☽ □
07 ♉ 16	51 07	09	07:06 ☽ ♂ ♃	01:22 ☽ □ ♀		15:53 ⊙ ⚹ ☽	21:44 ⊙ ⚹ ☽	06:56 ☽ ⚹ ⚷	12:56 ☽ □
21	49 58	11 23	10:48 ☽ ∠ ♀	03:19 ☽ ⚹ ♂	11 00:50 ☽ ♀ ♀	17:54 ☽ □ ♀	23:03 ☽ ± ☽	09:24 ☽ ∠ ♃	13:05 ☽ △
05 ♊ 56	10 14	50	16:29 ☽ ♂ ♀	05:40 ⊙ ♂ ♀	01:05 ☽ △ ♃	20:20 ☽ ♂		10:34 ☽ ⚹ ♃	13:15 ♀ △
19	34 01	17 19	21:00 ⊙ ♂° ☽	07:15 ☽ ⚹ ♃	03:55 ☽ △ ♀	23:41 ☽ ♂° ♂	19 00:14 ☽	12:32 ⊙ □ ☽	14:56 ♀ ⚻
				14:34 ☽ ∠	09:11 ☽ m		04:06 ☽ △ ♂	13:12 ☽ ∠ ♂	18:16 ☽ □
02 ♋ 44	41	18 45	2 00:37 ♀ ⚻ ♄	17:51 ☽ ∠ ♄	11:20 ⊙ ♀ ☽	15 01:11 ☽ ⚻ ♓	07:34 ⊙ ∠ ♀	13:35 ⊙ ± ♂	20:41 ☽ ♂
15	31 11	19 09	01:19 ☽ ⚻ ♀	17:57 ☽ ± ♀	13:57 ☽ ∠ ♄	05:45 ☽ ♀ ♓	12:12 ☽ ⚻	21:27 ☽ M	
27	57 37	18 34	12:40 ☽ ± ♂	18:55 ⊙ ♀	14:16 ☽ ⚹ ♂	08:38 ☽ ♀ ♀	12:38 ☽ ⚻ ♀	22:20 ☽ △ ♂	28 01:52 ⊙ ±
10 ♌ 08	26 17	07	12:47 ☽ ♂° ♀	21:42 ☽ ∠ ♀	14:39 ⊙ ⚻ ♀	10:56 ☽ ⚻	13:31 ☽ ♀ ♀		03:53 ☽
22	08 04	14 54	17:09 ☽ □ ♀	23:23 ♀ ± ♄	20:47 ☽ ♀	14:20 ☽ ♂ ♀	14:00 ⊙ D	24 02:09 ☽ ⚻ ♓	06:58 ☽ ♂
04 ♍ 00	33 12	04	19:32 ☽ □ ♀		21:51 ☽ ⚻ ♂	17:02 ☽ ⚹ ♀	23:52 ⊙ ∠ ♂	03:10 ☽ ♀ ♄	07:28 ⊙ ±
15	49 23	08 46	21:07 ♀ ⚻ ♓	7 02:32 ☽ ♀		21:41 ☽ ± ♀	23:59 ☽ ♂ ♓	05:15 ☽ ∠ ♂	09:59 ♀
27	37 29	05 08	23:33 ☽ ♂ ♂	04:57 ☽ △ ♂	12 03:28 ☽ ♀ ♃	16 01:11 ☽ ± ♀	23:59 ☽	14:33 ☽ ∠ ♃	15:31 ☽ ∠
09 ♎ 27	15	01 N 18		06:52 ☽ ♀ ♃	08:37 ☽ □ ♀	10:38 ☽ ⚻ ♓		17:43 ♀ R	20:45 ⊙ ∠
				09:09 ⊙ △ ☽	10:03 ☽ ⚹ ♓	13:09 ☽ □ ♀	20 03:24 ☽ ± ♀	20:07 ☽ ∠	
PHASES ⊙ ◑			3 01:40 ☽ ⚹ ⚷	17:38 ☽ ∠ ♀	11:10 ☽ ∠ ♀	14:24 ☽ ♂° ♀	08:00 ☽ ♀ ☽	22:12 ☽ □ ♀	29 02:48 ☽ ♂°
:m Phase Long.			02:09 ☽ ⚻ ♀	20:15 ☽ ∠ ♀	13:09 ☽ ± ♂	17:32 ☽ △	10:33 ☽ ♀ ♀	:44 ☽ ⚻ ♓	06:41 ☽ ♀
			10:41 ☽ ♀	22:47 ☽ △ ♂	13:09 ☽ ± ♂	18:33 ☽ ∠	11:11 ⊙ ♈	:57 ☽ ⚹ ♓	21:57 ☽ ∠
:00 ⊙ 11 ♍ 26			10:51 ☽ ♀ ♄	23:15 ☽ ⚹ ♄	15:05 ☽ ∠ ♂	18:57 ⊙ ♀	13:24 ☽ ⚻ ♂	25 :58 ☽ ♀ ☽	
:50 ◑ 19 ♐ 34			16:30 ☽ ⚹ ♂		16:06 ☽ ⚹ ♓	20:31 ☽ ♀	14:11 ☽ △ ♄	:49 ☽ △ ⚷	30 01:22 ♀ ♂°
:57 ● 26 ♓ 21			19:17 ☽ ∠ ♃	8 02:00 ☽ ♂ ♓	18:52 ☽ ± ♃	22:23 ☽ ⚻	17:58 ☽ ♂° ♀	:41 ☽ ♀ ♂	01:24 ☽ □
:32 ◐ 03 ♋ 02			20:45 ♓ m	10:39 ☽ ∠	23:11 ☽ ⚻ ♃		20:37 ☽ ± ♀	10:08 ☽ m	01:55 ☽ ♀
:15 ⊙ 11 ♎ 03			4 02:05 ☽ S	12:47 ☽ □ ♂	23:46 ☽ ⚻ ♒	17 00:42 ☽ ♈	21:43 ☽ □ ♂	13:24 ☽ ⚹ ♓	07:02 ☽ ⚹
			08:07 ☽ ♀ ♀	14:37 ☽ ♀ ♀		04:49 ☽ ⚻ ♀			07:35 ☽ △

The aspectarian is a section in the ephemerides that lists the aspects of the day. Planets are in aspect to each other when there are specific angular distances between them. The aspectarian is an indispensable source of information when working with progressions.

astrological knowledge will develop. It is also helpful to know the polarities—pairings of opposites, e.g. Aries and Libra. If you look up 21 March 1979, the aspectarian for that day includes: 05.23 ⊙ (Sun) ♈ (Aries). This means that in 1979 the Sun moved into Aries at 05.23 GMT on 21 March. However, if you look up 21 March 1980, you will see that the aspectarian does not list the Sun's ingress on that day. To find where the Sun was in

1980, you have to look a day either side. This year the Sun ingressed into Aries on 20 March, and the aspectarian for that day includes: 11.11 ⊙ (Sun) ♈ (Aries). This means that in 1980 the Sun moved into Aries at 11.11 GMT on 20 March.

SIGNS, ELEMENTS, AND MODES

I have given the main characteristics of the elements and modes below but I find providing lists of keywords as a means to

ELEMENTS OR TRIPLICITIES *There are three signs for each element, hence the notation triplicities.*	KEY CHARACTERISTICS
FIRE *Aries, Leo, Sagittarius*	*energy, warmth, vision, intuition*
EARTH *Taurus, Virgo, Capricorn*	*sensuality, practicality, fertility*
AIR *Gemini, Libra, Aquarius*	*thought, intellect, ideas, interaction*
WATER *Cancer, Scorpio, Pisces*	*sensitivity, feelings, instinct*

interpret combinations of signs, elements, and modes can be misleading. For example, we associate earth signs with practicality, but this shows how a keyword can place the astrologer in a symbolic straitjacket. Practicality is just one characteristic of earth and there are many impractical earth people.

As with Sun signs, it is important to learn from generalizations but also to recognize their limitations. Being open to how each sign has its own particular way of belonging to its element and mode fosters a "symbolic attitude"—an ability to regard symbolism as something that will speak to you rather than as something that exists as pure, objective fact, totally knowable in advance. Symbolism is about an infinite range of inherent meanings and not about a finite number of possibilities. In other words, it is dynamic, and this principle lies at the heart of accurate interpretation.

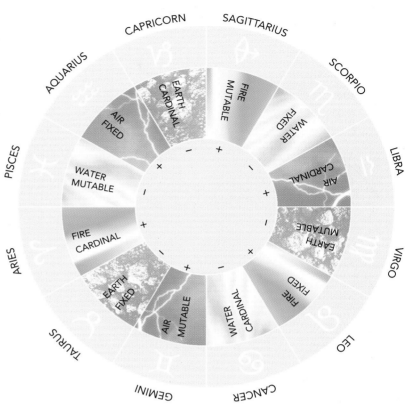

MODES OR QUADRUPLICITIES
There are four signs for each mode, hence the notation quadruplicities.

KEY CHARACTERISTICS

CARDINAL *Aries, Cancer, Libra, Capricorn*

This mode represents the element in its most concentrated or active form. It is associated with push, energy, and enterprise.

FIXED *Taurus, Leo, Scorpio, Aquarius*

As the name suggests, this mode represents the element in its least changeable form. It is associated with stability or stubbornness.

MUTABLE *Gemini, Virgo, Sagittarius, Pisces*

Sometimes called "common," this mode represents the element at its most fluid. It is associated with change and the dissemination of energy.

Aries

RULING PLANET MARS

GLYPH ♈

ELEMENT AND MODE CARDINAL FIRE

KEY PHRASE I AM

Aries is the first sign of the zodiac—and that is the biggest clue to the Aries personality. A typical Aries loves to come first in all things and is not remotely interested in second place. He or she wants to be your favorite person, the greatest love of your life, top of the class, head of the office, and the winner of games.

Aries people are ruled by Mars, the god of war, and they simply can't go into battle without being competitive. However, the desire to win and excel can be obvious or subtle, and is as much for personal satisfaction as for public acclaim. Aries is the sign of the ego and can be "self"-ish, but this is due to the need to assert, express, and define its own sense of self before it is able to turn its attention toward others.

As leaders of the zodiacal pack, Aries individuals are trailblazers, initiators, and pioneers. Their nature is spontaneous, direct, immediate, effective, and positive. They prefer action to thought or deliberation and are brilliant at simply getting things done with no messing around. They thrive on achievement, and other people's laziness, ineptitude, or prevarication can drive them crazy.

Aries rules the head and many people of this sign have a strong profile, with high cheekbones and a firm jaw. Headaches, migraines, or injuries to the head or face are common afflictions when an Aries person is under stress or in crisis.

DEFENDER OF THE WEAK

Not surprisingly, then, patience is not an Aries strength, with one notable exception, and that is when Aries takes up someone else's cause. Aries people have no time for those who won't help themselves but they are incomparable defenders of the underdog. Many Aries people are to be found in the caring professions such as social work or human rights.

Impatience in other areas, however, highlights the Aries lesson in life, which is to learn that the ego cannot always be gratified instantaneously. Aries people are generally expert at getting their own way in a "let's compromise and do it my way" fashion, but unless this is combined with giving in gracefully sometimes, they risk loneliness and a lack of positive regard.

Taurus

RULING PLANET VENUS

GLYPH

ELEMENT AND MODE FIXED EARTH

KEY PHRASE I POSSESS

After the realization of the self as personified in Aries, Taurus brings us back down to earth and connects us to the physical world. Taurus is ruled by Venus, or Aphrodite, the goddess of love, who also rules money, sustenance, and earthly pleasures. A typical Taurean is Venusian in nature—sensual, appetitive, and materialistic. Whatever a Taurean can see, smell, touch, taste, or feel is there to be enjoyed.

Taureans are especially lovers of good food, and they can sometimes have a struggle with their weight. Their sensuality also means that they are devotees of beauty, style, and comfort. When they get into that famous Taurean bad mood, which generally lasts about three days, they can at least be miserable in luxury—or go shopping. It was probably a Taurus person who coined the phrase "retail therapy." But in many ways the most fulfilled Taureans are those who develop their sixth sense and discover that there is more to life than the other five senses reveal, as exemplified by their opposite sign of Scorpio, the sign that rules all that is hidden or mysterious.

The second clue to the Taurean's own brand of earthiness is that it is fixed. A typical Taurean is at his or her best when feeling grounded and safe, and he or she is not known for being a risk taker. Taureans like to test the water before they jump in and hate to be pushed or rushed in any way. There is resistance to change, even extreme stubbornness, but a typical Taurean is naturally cautious and values familiarity and security. Avoiding risk, however, fosters a tendency to leave things the same for too long, and Taurus people need to be careful about getting stuck in a rut, whether this is a relationship, job, or lifestyle. Inertia can be the biggest enemy.

LIVE AND LET LIVE

However, the Taurus temperament is mostly placid, kind, peaceable, and sensible. Taureans tend to live and let live rather than find fault, mostly because they are tolerant, slow to anger, and possess a droll and often hilarious sense of humor. However, if pushed too far, the Taurean temper can explode, and the raging bull can be pretty fearsome. Once provoked into anger or distress, Taureans are slow to forgive, as nobody disturbs their physical, mental, or emotional equilibrium without paying a price. The positive side to this fixity is a ferocious willpower and absolute loyalty to loved ones, although they need to guard against possessiveness.

Taurus rules the throat, and there are many famous singers born under this sign, with very rich, sensual, or gravelly voices. Taureans are susceptible to bad throats, tonsillitis, or laryngitis when unhappy or under stress.

Gemini

RULING PLANET MERCURY

GLYPH ♊

ELEMENT AND MODE MUTABLE AIR

KEY PHRASE I SPEAK

The symbol of the twins immediately suggests duality, and this is the most important characteristic of the Gemini nature. Duality often manifests as some kind of "doubling up" theme, anything from two jobs, two cars, two dogs, to two marriages. This duality can become multiplicity, and the two or more theme often shows on a day-to-day level, such as an inability to buy or own just one of anything.

Gemini's planet Mercury can, fittingly, be either masculine or feminine, and it rules the hands. This sign generally possesses dexterity, and a typical Gemini is a true multi-tasker, at home with doing more than one thing at a time, mentally and physically. Gemini's hands may be busy with a certain task, but his or her mind is almost certainly elsewhere, solving a work problem or planning next year's vacation. A typical Gemini will also gesticulate in conversation in order to express him or herself. Gemini also rules the arms, shoulders, lungs, and the nervous system, and many Geminis are excitable or run off nervous energy.

Geminis are the tricksters of the zodiac. They love practical jokes, clever wit, and disguise, often smudging the line between playfulness and deceit. They are also the Peter Pan of the zodiac, and the typical Gemini keeps age at bay, naturally or through artifice, and refuses to grow up.

THE GREAT COMMUNICATOR
In mythology, Mercury is also Hermes, the winged messenger of the gods, and Gemini is the sign of communication, as expressed in its key phrase "I speak." Journalism, writing, any kind of media work, or jobs involving driving are all classic Gemini occupations. Geminis love to talk, gossip, and debate, often playing the devil's advocate to liven up the proceedings. They have

butterfly minds, flitting from one subject to the next, and can be mines of both useful and useless information. They are inquisitive, often witty, always on the move, and almost impossible to pin down, so Geminis are often the jack of all trades and master of none. To specialize requires a concerted effort and Geminis are more likely to adopt the policy that variety is the spice of life, turning their hand to whatever comes their way. This also avoids boredom, a Gemini's idea of hell.

Geminis also think very fast on their feet, especially if they are cornered. As the sign of mutable air, these individuals are quick, clever, and elusive and can vanish into thin air if necessary.

Cancer

RULING PLANET THE MOON

GLYPH

ELEMENT AND MODE CARDINAL WATER

KEY PHRASE I SECURE

As with all the water signs, Cancer individuals are sensitive, although first impressions may not reveal this. The sign of the crab has a hard shell, so the exterior that is presented to the world can be pretty tough, but don't be fooled. The shell is a neat device for self-protection that successfully conceals the soft center and vulnerable underbelly, and can also be a retreat when life gets too much.

Cancerians do not like confrontation. Like the crab, they tend to adopt the sideways approach, going quietly through the back door wherever possible, and in life's battles they tend to choose flight rather than fight. Their nature is indirect, cautious, and evasive, sometimes slow or hesitant, but this doesn't mean that they don't get results. They simply get them in their own good time and without anyone else really noticing. Patience and tenacity are their greatest assets.

CARING BUT CHANGEABLE
Cancerians are experts at looking after others as well as themselves. They are ruled by the Moon, which symbolizes mothering, home, and family, and these concerns rank high in Cancerian priorities. It is unusual for them not to get married and have children, and they are generally fiercely protective of their loved ones.

The rulership of the Moon gives other clues to the Cancer personality. Just as the Moon presents a different shape every night, so do the Cancerian moods wax and wane, from clownish humor to downright "crabby." These individuals are retentive and usually have excellent memories, but their reluctance to be open can tip over into extreme secretiveness, especially when it comes to guarding their innermost feelings, and then they have to be coaxed out of their shells.

The Moon rules Cancer and also rules habits, and a typical Cancerian is a creature of habit. Cancerians stick to their own systems and routines and they dislike disruption, especially at short notice.

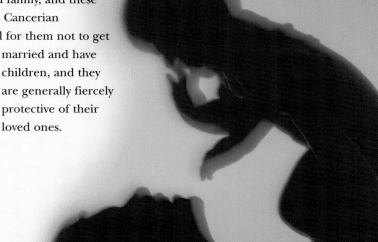

Leo

RULING PLANET THE SUN

GLYPH ♌

ELEMENT AND MODE FIXED FIRE

KEY PHRASE I CREATE

Roll out the red carpet and sound the fanfare, royalty is here. The sign of the Lion is quite simply the king of the zodiac, and Leo people exude stateliness, sometimes haughtiness. You can often recognize a Leo by a regal bearing and a way of holding court, or even just by the way he or she walks into a room. Leos value personal pride and dignity and announce themselves.

Leo is the only sign ruled by the Sun and, just as the Sun is the center of our galaxy, so are Leo individuals the center of their own universes. They have a knack for being at the heart of things and love to be the center of attention. Performers or show-offs, Leos are at their most entertaining when playing to an audience. They claim attention, blatantly or quietly, as an unconscious response to playing the hated second fiddle.

SUN WORSHIPPER

Leos love the sun, physically and metaphorically, and will turn their faces to the warmth of good feeling and bask in the rays. Some Leos have a tendency to indolence, but usually in quite a contented way. But Leos who feel unneeded or unappreciated can sink into inertia, leading to depression or illness. More than any other sign Leos thrive on unconditional regard and wither without it. There is nothing sadder than an unloved Leo.

Leo individuals are at their best when they are Top Cat, and need to be self-employed, the boss, or in a position of responsibility. They will find success in any role that allows them to exploit their talent for bold self-expression and creativity. They are natural organizers but they can be bossy or overbearing, taking over at the drop of a hat. The Leo lesson is to allow space for other people's needs, opinions, and egos.

Leo rules the back, especially the spine, and people born under this sign either have excellent posture or suffer from back problems. A Leo can be the backbone of his or her family or workplace. This sign also rules the heart, so Leos can be big-hearted, speak from the heart, and act on heartfelt feelings.

Virgo

RULING PLANET MERCURY

GLYPH ♍

ELEMENT AND MODE MUTABLE EARTH

KEY PHRASE I SERVE

A typical Virgo will adopt the policy that, if something is worth doing, then it is worth doing faultlessly, or not at all. Here is the perfectionist of the zodiac, and those born under this sign can easily get a reputation for being critical or over-demanding. Their saving grace is that Virgos' highest standards are almost certainly the ones they set for themselves—and it's a full-time job living up to them.

Virgo is aligned to service, as expressed in its key phrase "I serve," and embodies a strong work ethic, but sometimes at the expense of other areas of life. Workaholism is a Virgo trap, even to the extent of creating work that is not really necessary. A Virgo friend once told me that her boss had returned work to her because it was too detailed and she then had to spend hours simplifying it. Not being able to see the wood for the trees is a common Virgo problem, simply because nothing escapes his or her attention.

Virgos often suffer from an inner turmoil, which may be hard to spot as their outer worlds are usually highly organized. Virgo homes, for example, are generally neat, minimal, and sanitized, with a place for everything and everything in its place.

SEEKER AFTER PERFECTION

This sign at its best has an unparalleled talent for discrimination, precision, and a keen eye for detail, so unsurprisingly this is the sign of skills and crafts. Such expertise requires patience and painstaking exactitude, which are a typical Virgo's forte. So, take note that a Virgo hates to be wrong or criticized after expending so much time and energy on getting it right.

This sign rules the intestines and Virgos need a carefully balanced diet. Some Virgos have a tendency to hypochondria or can get ill through anxiety. This is also the sign of health and many Virgos work in caring professions.

The exacting Virgo mind generally presents a serious front to the world, often as a result of being afraid to make mistakes, but often this masks an intelligent and sharp sense of humor.

Any quest for perfection is not necessarily doomed to failure, but it is certainly a path that is beset with pitfalls. Expecting too much from others leads Virgos inevitably to disappointment and reinforces their suspicion that no one is ever good enough. One of the Virgo lessons in life is to learn that to err is human, to forgive divine, especially when it comes to love. An anxious Virgo will be over-analytical at best, nagging and nit-picking at worst, and has to be careful not to destroy the thing he or she is trying to correct and perfect.

Libra

RULING PLANET VENUS

GLYPH ⎓

ELEMENT AND MODE CARDINAL AIR

KEY PHRASE I RELATE

Many people instantly equate the sign of the Scales with balance and harmony. While these are undoubtedly Libran issues, the most important symbolism of this sign lies in the fact that it is the seventh sign of the zodiac and therefore the opposite sign to Aries, the sign of the ego and individuality. Libra represents the opposite principle, the importance of the significant other and all key relationships.

This is the sign of partnership, and a typical Libran hates to do things alone or to be without a relationship for too long. Librans need to share intimate companionship and love, to bounce their thoughts and ideas off others, or simply to collect different views and opinions. "What do you think?" is the classic Libran question, and on the plus side, their powers of negotiation, arbitration, and compromise are second to none. But Librans fear loneliness more than any other sign and cease to function effectively without input and support from their world at large but especially from a partner. The classic Libran trap is to become involved with someone too quickly or to stay in the wrong relationship for the sake of it—the "someone is better than no one" policy.

Libra is ruled by Venus and is the sign of beauty, balance, and harmony. If the pursuit of romance in love and life is fruitless, Librans will sink into despondency, reacting with passive resistance to helping hands.

STUCK FOR CHOICES

Another saying associated with Libra is "I can't be bothered," and this sign is sometimes called "Lazy Libra." However, what may seem to be laziness is usually more often a form of mental paralysis. The scales of Libra are famous for symbolizing the weighing up of pros and cons, but Librans are so good at seeing every angle and viewpoint that the result is often confusion or uncertainty rather than clarity. Making a decision or a choice is not always the problem—but believing that it is the right one and sticking to it is another matter. Librans are also quick to assume blame or guilt and will apologize when they have done nothing wrong.

In the physical body Libra rules the kidneys. Librans need to flush out the old and to keep their lives moving. Illnesses may sometimes arise from inactivity.

Scorpio

RULING PLANETS MARS, PLUTO

GLYPH ♏

ELEMENT AND MODE FIXED WATER

KEY PHRASE I REGENERATE

Scorpios have a reputation for being mysterious and complicated, a reputation they do little to refute. As the sign of fixed water, Scorpio individuals can present a frozen front but they are actually far from glacial. "Still waters run deep," and the Scorpio fathomless expression expertly masks hidden depths, which are teeming with life.

There is nothing superficial about this sign, and a typical Scorpio lives life with enormous intensity. Feelings are passionate, and often black and white—love or hate, good or bad—and it is difficult for them to accept other people's indifference. Scorpios have to learn and acquire the easygoing tolerance of their opposite sign of Taurus.

Scorpio is the sign of the sixth sense and its insights can border on the psychic. Along with their own fascinating depths, Scorpios are intrigued by things that are

hidden, mysterious, or taboo. They are co-ruled by Pluto, god of the underworld, and Scorpios love to dig under the surface and tease out mysteries. From secrets to psychoanalysis, Scorpio is the sleuth of the zodiac. Scorpios want to know what makes you tick, and they won't rest until they do. Many Scorpios are found in the world of therapy and healing.

Scorpio's traditional ruler is Mars, the god of war, and a typical Scorpio is forceful, determined, and thorough. Scorpio's all-or-nothing

The ability to destroy is the flip side to Scorpio's strength: regeneration. Scorpio rules the cycle of life and death, hence its reputation for being sexually powerful. It also rules the reproductive system and illnesses associated with it.

approach to life means that he or she is not always the easiest of people to deal with and Scorpios have to learn how to compromise rather than intimidate, to use their power constructively and positively. It is too easy for them to take control of situations and of other people.

VENGEFUL STING

The scorpion carries a sting in its tail and it is true that this can be a jealous and vengeful sign. With their passionate feelings Scorpios find it almost impossible to make light of things, least of all their own hurts, and the need for revenge is virtually a knee-jerk reaction. However, they are just as likely to wound themselves in the process. Scorpios also know how to walk away from one way of life and start again, often from scratch.

Sagittarius

RULING PLANET JUPITER

GLYPH

ELEMENT AND MODE MUTABLE FIRE

KEY PHRASE I SEEK

There are many strings to the Archer's bow and typical Sagittarians will fire their arrows and pursue them with energy and enthusiasm. The arrows symbolize that which is sought—sometimes they hit the mark and sometimes they don't. However, this is the sign of the traveler and it is often the journey itself that is more important than the final goal or target.

Sagittarius rules all things foreign and those born under this sign often feel more at home when abroad than in their country of birth. Physically and mentally restless, this is also the sign of the future and the tendency to look ahead is the root of Sagittarius' famous optimism. There is a certain childlike trust in the world, which is often justified, albeit often at the 11th hour. Nevertheless, a Sagittarian lesson in life is to learn to appreciate the here and now rather than looking to the unknown.

LARGER THAN LIFE
Sagittarians are often exuberant and their tendency to exaggerate and to do things to excess can make them rather overwhelming. They are known for their bluntness and are often unaware of the anguish they may be causing. Sagittarius needs to learn the more subtle arts of language from its opposite sign of Gemini.

In the physical body, Sagittarius rules the thighs, buttocks, and especially the hips. Sagittarians tend to walk with a long swinging stride and many accomplished sports people are born under this sign.

This sign also rules religion and the law and other typical Sagittarian values are justice, truth, and honesty. If you want to fan the flames of the Sagittarian temper, accuse them of lying. But, for good or ill, there is nothing hidden with this sign and, mostly, what you see is what you get. The only thing that is private is sadness, and tears will be shed into a pillow or on the shoulder of a friend while the rest of the world sees only cheerfulness.

Sagittarius is also the sign of the higher mind. It is the philosopher and teacher of the zodiac, and the pursuit of wisdom and search for meaning are just as important as new places and experiences. However, there is a risk of leaving plans and projects unfinished if something new beckons.

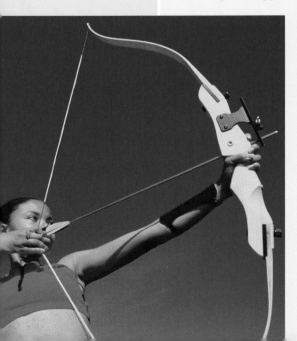

Capricorn

DECEMBER 22–JANUARY 20

RULING PLANET SATURN

GLYPH ♑

ELEMENT AND MODE CARDINAL EARTH

KEY PHRASE I MASTER

As the sign of the mountain goat, a typical Capricorn is hardy, steady, sure-footed, and purposeful. Capricorns know how to pick their way to the summit, always keeping their goal in sight, and hence this is the sign of ambition. This ambition takes many forms but it is not always of the burning kind. Capricorns love to have plans mapped out clearly to know what they are doing and why.

Everything with Capricorns has to have a point, whether it's redesigning the kitchen or empire-building, and they believe in the value of hard work, application, and discipline. The aim is always to build and achieve, but they tend to adopt the policy of slowly and surely rather than overnight success. Their powers of endurance keep them on track.

Capricorns are ruled by Saturn, the planet of boundaries, and they like to know where they stand. Personal privacy is important and guardedness can take the form of quiet reserve and humor. Capricorns are very careful of other people's boundaries, too, and prefer to build relationships gradually rather than assuming intimacy too quickly. They are courteous and mindful, treading carefully around other people's feelings and opinions.

TIME ALONE

Capricorn is also the sign of authority, duty, and responsibility, too much of which is often experienced early in life. It is not uncommon for Capricorns to assume adult responsibilities while still in their teens, or even miss out on a proper childhood altogether, and these individuals know all about loneliness. They sometimes have a tendency to retreat from the crowd, which ranges from needing time alone to living an almost hermit-like existence, and have to learn the skills of nurture and nourishment of their opposite sign of Cancer.

Capricorn rules the bones, especially the knees and teeth. Those born under this sign often have excellent bone structure, producing striking faces. This sign also rules the skin. Many Capricorns have strong frames and are resilient, so this is not a sickly sign. However, Capricorn rules difficult-to-treat afflictions such as osteoporosis, arthritis, and psoriasis.

Aquarius

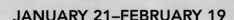

RULING PLANETS SATURN, URANUS

GLYPH

ELEMENT AND MODE FIXED AIR

KEY PHRASE I UNDERSTAND

Aquarius may be the sign of the Water Bearer but it nevertheless belongs to air, the element of the mind, and many people of this sign are of above average intelligence. Aquarius is the sign of intellect, ideology, social and political concerns, and humanitarian or ecological causes.

Aquarius is objective and concerns itself with any issues that affect society, the planet, and the world at large. Its opposite sign of Leo represents the power and creativity of the individual, but Aquarius looks above the concept of self in favor of the group. The paradox of this sign lies in the fact that Aquarians prize their own individuality and often feel "different" from the rest of the world, even from an early age. The ability to detach is a double-edged sword and can be a handicap when it comes to fitting in and forging personal relationships.

Aquarius rules the legs, especially the ankles, and circulation. This sign often suffers from the cold and needs to create warmth and coziness in its life.

UNEASY INTIMACY
Aquarians are often easily embarrassed or uncomfortable with displays of emotion and can be disconnected from their own feelings. Intimacy does not come easily to them, even though they may secretly crave it. A matter-of-fact approach or superiority about their "differentness" can easily give the wrong impression of needing nobody, which can then result in their feeling unneeded because others do not worry that they may not be able to cope. Aquarians have to learn the art of

seduction and courtship from their opposite sign of Leo, who simply claims attention as a birthright.

The sign of Aquarius rules relationships with a small "r," including the social circle and colleagues. More than any other sign, Aquarians need a meeting of minds, and their most successful romantic relationships tend to spring from friendship rather than instant attraction. Aquarians also tend to keep ex-lovers and partners as friends whenever possible.

The rulership of Aquarius is shared by two planets: Saturn and Uranus. The symbolism of Saturn describes the Aquarian who is serious, disciplined, organized, deadly logical, and highly systematic. Most Aquarians are compulsive list-makers and place great value on their own way of doing things. In this respect they need to guard against inflexibility.

The Uranian symbolism describes the other type of Aquarian who is the rebel with or without a cause, the misfit, or the mad professor—unusual, eccentric, quirky, and way ahead of his or her time. Both types believe that they are right.

Pisces

FEBRUARY 20–MARCH 20

RULING PLANETS JUPITER, NEPTUNE

GLYPH ♓

ELEMENT AND MODE MUTABLE WATER

KEY PHRASE I REDEEM

Pisces is co-ruled by Neptune, or Poseidon, god of the sea. It is a rare Piscean who does not feel a powerful affinity with the ocean, whether it's just to breathe the sea air, to live on a boat, to work on the water, or to enjoy a passion for water sports. Pisceans often struggle with the realities of day-to-day life. Like the sea their personalities are boundless, and they have a horror of being confined.

Pisceans like to be a big fish in a small pond rather than the other way around, but finding a sense of direction is their biggest challenge. Once they find their way upstream they can achieve great things, but until this turn is successfully made, a typical Pisces is aimless and adrift, the proverbial fish out of water.

Pisceans are highly sensitive. They are acutely receptive to other people's moods and can soak up undercurrents and atmospheres like sponges. A typical Piscean learns in this way, too, often just absorbing information rather than adopting a conscious approach. On the down-side, this sensitivity can make the world a cruel place, and Pisceans need to learn self-protection. With no shell or sting, this water sign is vulnerable and easily wounded.

This sign rules the feet, and Pisceans are susceptible to problems in this area. Pisceans need to be careful around alcohol or drugs, as this can be the sign of addictive behavior.

TAKING SHAPE

A typical Piscean needs structure in life in order for his or her personality to take shape. Like water, Pisceans will take the shape of the vessel, fitting into other people's molds and expectations, and many actors are born under this sign. A typical Piscean lives on the interface between fantasy and reality and can lean toward escapism. The desire to please, and to rescue others, can lead to disillusionment in the impossible attempt to keep everyone happy.

A complete horoscope comprises of ten heavenly bodies—the Sun, Moon, Mercury, Venus, Mars, Jupiter, Saturn, Uranus, Neptune, and Pluto. As with the signs, each planet has its own dominion and symbolizes particular aspects of both our inner and outer worlds. Each planet also has certain signs in which it is traditionally empowered or weakened. Understanding how the nature of each planet is expressed and modified through each of the signs constitutes the foundation of chart interpretation.

THE PLANETS

INTRODUCING THE PLANETS

Everybody knows their Sun sign but when it comes to horoscopes there are ten planets in all to consider—the Sun, Moon, Mercury, Venus, Mars, Jupiter, Saturn, Uranus, Neptune, and Pluto. Each planet occupies a certain sign so, while our Sun sign can symbolize our essential self, we are all a combination of signs.

From the diagram on the opposite page you will see that there is a definite pattern of planets and signs. Both the Sun and the Moon rule one sign each. The other personal planets, from Mercury through to Saturn, rule two signs each, one masculine and one feminine.

Moving round the wheel on either side of the Sun and Moon you will find the Mercury signs of Gemini and Virgo, then the Venus signs of Taurus and Libra, then the Mars signs of Aries and Scorpio, then the Jupiter signs of Pisces and Sagittarius, finishing up at the top of the wheel with the Saturn-ruled signs of Aquarius and Capricorn. The beautiful symmetry of this pattern would be spoiled if we were to replace the traditional planets with the modern, more recently discovered ones, so Uranus, Neptune, and Pluto are assigned as co-rulers to Aquarius, Pisces, and Scorpio respectively.

One of the first steps in learning about the planets is to note how each has its own dominion, and then how the planets' symbolism is in sympathy and accord with the signs that they rule. We can then understand more easily their signs of detriment, exaltation, and fall, and these placings are covered in detail in the second half of this chapter.

Learning about the craft of horoscopes is a bit like peeling an onion—there are several layers to work through before you are able to convert the information into meaningful interpretation. (We will look at houses and aspects in the following chapter.) At this stage, it is helpful to note the following points:

◆ When a planet is well-placed this means that it is in a strong sign or house, or is in positive aspect to other planets, or a combination of these factors.

◆ When a planet is ill-placed—or afflicted—this means that it is either in a weak sign or house, or is in negative aspect to other planets, or a combination of these factors.

In addition to the ten planets there are two other traditional features of a horoscope—the Part of Fortune and the Moon's nodes—and modern astrology also now includes the recently discovered planet Chiron. I will look at these toward the end of this chapter.

In astrology all the signs are either masculine or feminine and the same applies to the planets: the Moon and Venus are feminine, while all the other planets are masculine. In practice, most astrologers would naturally refer to the Moon, as "She," Saturn as "He," and so on. In the following pages the planets are referred to as "it," but this choice has been made for linguistic purposes only. It is important to remember that the planets are always carriers of symbolism and not just astronomical objects.

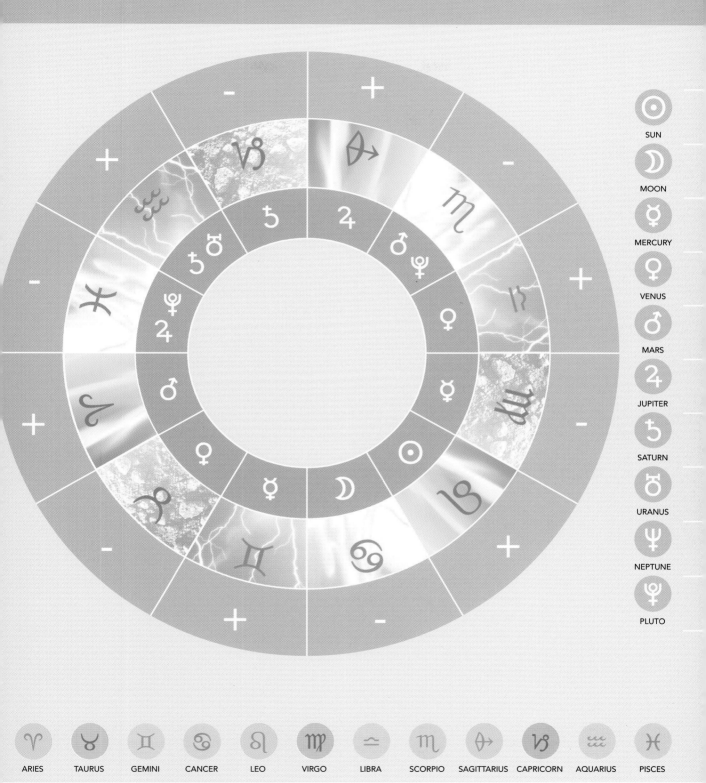

SUN
MOON
MERCURY
VENUS
MARS
JUPITER
SATURN
URANUS
NEPTUNE
PLUTO

ARIES TAURUS GEMINI CANCER LEO VIRGO LIBRA SCORPIO SAGITTARIUS CAPRICORN AQUARIUS PISCES

The Sun

SIGN OF DIGNITY LEO

COLORS GOLD, YELLOW, ORANGE

DAY OF THE WEEK SUNDAY

METAL GOLD

Once a year the Sun "travels" around the zodiac, so our birthday is our Solar Return, the day that the Sun returns to the same sign and degree as on the day we were born, hence "Many Happy Returns of the Day." The Sun is traditionally known as "The Lord of the Day" and, along with the Moon, is one of the "Lights"—the Sun being the light of the day, the Moon being the light of the night.

As Lord of the Day the Sun is masculine and can represent the father and, in a woman's horoscope, the partner and the kind of men to whom she is attracted.

At a universal level both the Sun and Leo are associated with royalty, majesty, stateliness, dignity, and authority. Strong Solar types exude seemingly boundless energy and vitality and share many of the positive Leo characteristics—generosity, courage, confidence, clarity of vision, loyalty, strength of character, and glowing health.

An afflicted Sun has the reverse of the above qualities, such as arrogance, attention-seeking, insecurity, lack of confidence, and a shaky sense of identity. Poor health and a lack of vitality can also be manifestations of an afflicted Sun.

YOUR ESSENTIAL SELF

As the source of being and illumination the Sun represents your day world, consciousness, and psychological purpose.

Wherever the other planets may be placed in the horoscope, the Sun symbolizes your essential self and who you are struggling to become. An Aries is always an Aries, a Libran is always a Libran, no matter what the Moon sign, for example, may be. If you were to repress your own Sun sign attributes, you would cease to shine, living only in other people's light—self-conscious, lifeless, or depressed. In claiming your own light you can embrace a healthy self-love and experience a sense of feeling integrated and centered. This is reflected in the Sun's glyph, the dot marking the center of the circle, symbolizing the point of consciousness from which all life will emanate.

The Sun rules the heart, general vitality and constitution, and the back—especially the spine. Strong Solar types tend to share the Leo characteristic of having either excellent posture or back problems. The Sun also rules the right eye in a man, the left eye in a woman.

The Moon

SIGN OF DIGNITY CANCER

COLORS SILVER, WHITE

DAY OF THE WEEK MONDAY

METAL SILVER

The Sun is arguably the most important part of our astrological identity but the Moon, by receiving the Sun's light, presents the same size disc in the sky. In fact, they are a perfect match, as can be witnessed at a total eclipse, the Moon's disc fitting exactly over the Sun's. This suggests that the Lights carry equal symbolic weight and are dyadic, that is, the two bodies together create a powerful unit.

The Moon is the swiftest moving body. It travels through the zodiac every 28 days, spending approximately two and a half days in each sign.

The Moon rules the stomach and our "gut" reactions. It also rules the breasts, the left eye in a man, and the right eye in a woman.

LUNAR SYMBOLISM
As Lady of the Night the Moon is feminine and can represent the mother and, in a man's horoscope, the partner and the kind of women to whom he is attracted. At a universal level it is a powerful symbol of womankind and feminine energy, and it rules motherhood, babies, childhood, and fertility. It is at its most fecund in its own sign of Cancer and the other water signs of Pisces and Scorpio, although the latter can often indicate gynecological problems. It is said to be barren in Gemini, Leo, and Virgo, but if the horoscope is otherwise favorable for children these placings do not preclude pregnancy.

The Moon's 28-day cycle taps us into the menstrual cycle, and its waxing and waning can be seen to symbolize conception, pregnancy, and birth. This pattern is also reflected in the three phases of the Moon—new, half moon, and full.

RULER OF THE NIGHT
If the Sun rules our conscious day world then the Moon speaks of our night world, the dominion of the unconscious, dreams, and all that is shadowy. It holds sway over our emotions, needs, and habitual responses. It receives light, continually presenting a different shape, and is receptive and changeable. Strong Lunar types share many positive Cancerian characteristics, such as sensitivity and the ability to nurture and protect.

Mercury

SIGNS OF DIGNITY GEMINI, VIRGO

COLORS MIXED OR MULTICOLORED

DAY OF THE WEEK WEDNESDAY

METAL QUICKSILVER

The Sun's closest traveling companion, Mercury is never found further than 27 degrees away from the Sun. For this reason, Mercury is rarely visible and the best time to see it is during a total eclipse. Like the Sun, Mercury takes approximately a year to travel through the zodiac so, in the horoscope, Mercury is always either in the same sign as the Sun or in the preceding or following sign.

In Greek mythology Mercury is Hermes, the winged messenger of the gods. Thus Mercury symbolizes everything to do with communication, as reflected in its better known masculine rulership of Gemini, the talker of the zodiac. Mercury also rules the exacting and perfection-seeking feminine sign of Virgo, as the other function of the mind is to analyze, define, and discriminate.

Language reveals but can also conceal so Mercury also rules that which is not verbalized, such as private thoughts, fantasies, or opinions. Depending on its condition in the horoscope, Mercury is lies or truth, open or secretive, provocative or non-confrontational. Mercury is also humor and the significator of magic. It rules the hands—and the quickness of the hand deceives the eye—so Mercury can be a thief as well as a magician.

The Mercurial type is mostly characterized by dexterity, cleverness, or quickness. This can manifest physically through manual labor and skills, or mentally, through intelligence. A common characteristic is expressiveness. Not surprisingly Mercury is often a strong feature in the horoscopes of singers and musicians, as well as the mercurial professions of writing, presenting, reporting, or research. Mercury also rules the realm of local travel or short journeys, and the means of transport—such as cars, buses, and bicycles.

Mercury rules the throat, lungs, and respiratory system. Its illnesses include speech impediments or problems with the mouth, tongue, or breathing. It also rules the arms, hands, shoulders, and nervous system, and illnesses related to them.

CURIOUS CONCEALER

As the planet of the mind Mercury is curious but, as it is also the planet of youth, its attention span is short. It speaks of breadth rather than depth and therefore rules early education rather than serious study. It is also our voice and everything to do with the written or spoken word—letters, telephones, conversation, ideas, books, the media, and so on.

Venus

SIGNS OF DIGNITY TAURUS, LIBRA

COLORS GREEN, WHITE

DAY OF THE WEEK FRIDAY

METAL COPPER

Known as the morning or evening star, Venus is visible just before sunrise or just after sunset. In traditional astrology it is known as the Lesser Benefic. Like Mercury it is to be found between the Earth and the Sun. It is never further away from the Sun than 46 degrees so, in the horoscope, it is always either in the same sign as the Sun or in one of the two preceding or following signs.

In Greek mythology Venus is Aphrodite, the goddess of love, from whose name comes the word "aphrodisiac," that which induces desire. From Venus' name comes the word "venereal," which literally means "of lust."

Venus is feminine and rules our world of love and all desires. Through it we experience joy, rapture, lust, and the nature of our sexuality. Venusian types are generally wonderful lovers, but they are also lovers of beauty, art, music, and food. Venus rules sensuality and earthly pleasures as discovered through the senses of touch, taste, smell, sight, and sound, as exemplified through its feminine sign of Taurus. In this sense it is the opposite principle to Mercury, as our physical appetites are a response to need and want rather than part of an analytical process. In fact, our most powerful desires drive out judgment—we all know that trying to reason with anyone in love is useless.

Beyond the initial stages of attraction and desire come the arts and skills needed to build meaningful relationships, so Venus' masculine sign is Libra, the sign of relating and partnership. Venus rules pairing, meetings, engagements, weddings, and unions of all kinds. It can also speak of those we love outside of a romantic relationship, such as close friends or family members. It especially rules women, as indicated by the glyph, which is the universal symbol for womankind. In a man's chart it can show the type of woman to whom he is attracted.

LOVING AND BEAUTIFUL

As the Lesser Benefic, Venus rules beauty, and its physical attributes are good looks, prettiness, dimples, softness, roundness, and a tendency to put on weight. It also rules beautifying, such as make-up, perfume, jewelry, and all adornments.

In personality it indicates a loving and affectionate nature, someone who is peaceable, sociable, and sometimes lazy. Venus rules amusement and enjoyment.

Venus rules the throat and kidneys. Blood sugar levels and diabetes are also Venus' domain. It also rules illnesses arising from sexual activity.

Mars

SIGNS OF DIGNITY ARIES, SCORPIO

COLOR RED

DAY OF THE WEEK TUESDAY

METAL IRON

The sequence of planets as seen from the Earth is the Moon, Mercury, Venus, the Sun, and now Mars. The further away from the Sun the greater the planet's orbit and Mars takes two years to make its circuit of the zodiac. In traditional astrology Mars is known as the Lesser Malefic. In Greek mythology Mars is Ares, the god of war.

Mars symbolizes everything to do with how we go into battle and handle the cut and thrust of life, as reflected in its masculine rulership of Aries, the warrior of the zodiac. Mars is also the ruler of the feminine sign of Scorpio, which embodies Mars' qualities of determination and the subtle power of a strong personality.

ASSERTIVE AND URGENT

The nature of Mars is assertive, or aggressive and confrontational. It speaks of our sense of drive and urgency. As the god of war it rules strife, combat, conquerors, and weapons. Venus may speak of our sexuality in terms of enjoyment but Mars is the sex drive and the phallus. Where Venus is soft and slow, Mars is sharp and quick, and its nature is to attack, pierce, penetrate, cut, or wound. It rules knives and all who work with them, everything from the surgeon and his precise scalpel to the butcher and his hacksaw.

Mars rules the head and the nose, injuries to the face or skull, migraine or sinusitis, burning pain, burns, scars, fevers, rashes, infections, and inflammations.

In psychological terms Mars speaks of rage, how we do or don't get angry. An afflicted Mars can run the continuum from being quarrelsome or over-impulsive to being capable of cruelty or violence. Conversely, it can speak of one who is easily intimidated or unable to get angry. Attack may manifest as passive-aggressive or bullying behavior.

A well-placed Mars shares many of the positive characteristics of Aries, indicating a nature that is bold, courageous, and unafraid to take on a fight, either for the self or others. Anger can be channeled as a spur to action rather than being destructive. But Mars at its best is purposeful, an achiever and self-starter, and a force to be reckoned with.

Mars' color red symbolizes anger and passion but also heat in other guises. Its foods are hot, spicy, or bitter, and its plants are prickly, sharp, or stinging.

4 Jupiter

SIGNS OF DIGNITY SAGITTARIUS, PISCES

COLORS GREEN, PURPLE, DEEP BLUES

DAY OF THE WEEK THURSDAY

METAL TIN

Jupiter spends approximately one year in each sign so it takes 12 years to make its circuit of the zodiac. In traditional astrology Jupiter is known as the Greater Benefic. In Greek mythology Jupiter is Zeus, the supreme deity. It is also known as Jove, root of the word "jovial," and Jupiterian types are often recognizably cheerful.

Through its Sagittarius connection, Jupiter rules the hips, the pelvis, the thighs, and the sciatic nerve. It also rules the blood, the liver, and illnesses that arise from excess and too much of the good life.

Jupiter signifies the opposite principle to Mercury, as illustrated by the fact that Mercury is weak in Jupiter's own signs (Sagittarius and Pisces) and Jupiter is weak in Mercury's signs (Gemini and Virgo). Mercury rules details and the smaller picture, whereas Jupiter rules the grand scheme of things. As the king of the gods, Jupiter's main characteristic is largeness and its nature is to enlarge and expand.

LARGER THAN LIFE

Jupiter literally rules the world and it is the natural significator of all things foreign and long-distance travel. Jupiterian types are often physically large, larger than life, or characterized by itchy feet and a horror of being restricted in any way, characteristics that are often found in both of Jupiter's signs, Sagittarius and Pisces. They will always push the boundaries, physically or mentally, and are at their happiest when roaming, exploring, and learning. Jupiter rules higher education and the concerns of the higher mind, in particular justice, truth, freedom, religion, and philosophy, as embodied in the Sagittarius archetype. Jupiter professions are teaching, law, the clergy, charities, human rights, and sometimes politics.

This concern with the serious issues of life lends an earnestness to the Jupiterian type, so there is a risk of being didactic or righteous. However, the positive personality traits of Jupiter are generosity, humanity, friendliness, and optimism. A well-placed Jupiter also signifies a trust and faith in life and a belief that things always happen for a reason.

An afflicted Jupiter can signify someone who is joyless, mean, or fearful. Or there may be a tendency to place too much faith in Fate, which leads to an abdication of personal responsibility. Jupiter signifies enthusiasm, but carelessness or wastefulness are the flip side of its exuberance. This planet also rules opportunity, and blessings in disguise come under Jupiter's domain. Jupiter luck is often of the 11th-hour variety, a last-minute vindication of faith.

♄ Saturn

SIGNS OF DIGNITY CAPRICORN, AQUARIUS

COLORS BLACK, GRAY

DAY OF THE WEEK SATURDAY

METAL LEAD

As the most remote planet of the Solar system known to ancient astronomy, Saturn is the last of the "personal" planets. In traditional astrology it is known as the Greater Malefic. It takes just under 30 years to make a circuit of the zodiac. In Greek mythology Saturn is Chronos, the Greek word for time. Saturn rules time, aging, and their effects.

Saturn is known as Father Time, and is concerned with old age, boundaries, limitations, and death. This is further illustrated in the fact that Saturn is the enemy of the Sun and Moon, the Lights of life, being weak in their signs of dignity—Leo and Cancer respectively.

Not surprisingly, then, Saturn is easily associated with fear, gloom, and despondency, and, in the words of astrologer Liz Greene, "even his virtues are rather dreary—self-control, tact, thrift, caution." But Saturn is part of the astrological pattern. It has its own role and dominion, and is as crucial to the overall scheme as the other planets.

Saturn rules bones, especially the teeth and knees, the feet, the spleen, and the skin, so conditions such as psoriasis or eczema are Saturnian.

BOUNDARIES AND LIMITS

Saturn is a response to Jupiter's galloping boundlessness, as illustrated by the fact that Saturn is weak in Jupiter's strongest sign of Cancer and Jupiter is weak in

Saturn's own sign of dignity, Capricorn. Without Saturn we would have no boundaries. If Jupiter is "yes," Saturn is "no," telling us when to stop and how to mature through learning the purpose of self-denial and delaying of gratification. Through Saturn we learn our limitations, the greatest of which is our mortality, and that we have a finite length of time in which to fulfill our life's purpose. Thus Saturn is the planet of ambition, goals, and achievement, as embodied in his feminine rulership of Capricorn. It signifies the qualities needed to reach our goals—not just fight (Mars) or luck (Jupiter), but hard work, discipline, and perseverance.

Other positive characteristics of the Saturnian type are what may be termed the good old-fashioned values of courtesy, decorum, and propriety. Strong Saturnian types exude gravitas and take life seriously.

Uranus

SIGN OF DIGNITY AQUARIUS

COLORS GREEN, SKY BLUE, METALLIC BLUE

DAY OF THE WEEK NONE

METAL URANIUM

Uranus is the co-ruler of Aquarius, whose traditional ruler is Saturn. It takes between 76–84 years to make its circuit of the zodiac. Uranus was discovered in 1781, coinciding with the French and American revolutions, and the industrial revolution in England.

Astrologer Neil Spencer writes that, "the very nature of a planet's discovery has also been reckoned to echo its astrological principle." In accord with its era, Uranus speaks of liberty and human rights, rebellion, and social and technological advancement. Today, Uranus rules computers, satellite television, electricity, and machinery or inventions that revolutionize work and labor.

Uranus also rules socialism, and the horoscope for Britain's Labour Party is ruled by the Moon at 10 degrees Aquarius, in a positive aspect to Uranus. Prime Minister Tony Blair's Moon is at 11 degrees Aquarius, showing him to be at home as leader of the Labour Party.

Uranus rules dissociation, from schizophrenia to the "split" in all of us, the part of our psyche that disowns or denies all that is uncomfortable or undesirable.

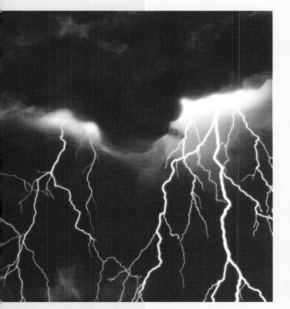

REBEL OF THE ZODIAC
Uranus symbolizes the rebel and is a direct response to Saturn's austerity. Saturn plays by the rules, but Uranus says that rules are there to be broken or challenged. Saturn is sensible, Uranus throws caution to the winds. Its nature is innovative, explosive, and unexpected, and it shatters the boundaries imposed by Saturn, scorning authority and convention. Uranus rules accidents, shocks, and all that is unpredictable. In mythology it is the sky god and it rules all that comes "out of the blue." In the natural world Uranus rules earthquakes and electrical storms.

The typical Uranian type is primarily different. He or she may be fascinating, brilliant, eccentric, chaotic, unstable, a wild child, or a genius, but is always unconventional or original, signifying many Aquarian characteristics.

Neptune

SIGN OF DIGNITY PISCES

COLORS BLACK, SEA GREEN

DAY OF THE WEEK NONE

METAL NONE

The co-ruler of Pisces, whose traditional ruler is Jupiter, Neptune takes approximately 170 years to make its circuit of the zodiac. Neptune was discovered in 1846 and the major developments of this era, such as photography and film, aptly echo the symbolism of this outer planet.

Psychologically, Neptune is the opposite principle to Uranus. Uranus divides and separates but Neptune signifies fusion and the collapsing of boundaries, without which we would never experience falling in love or empathy. The Neptunian struggle is learning how to replace boundaries.

The world of photographs and movies was born in Neptune's era. The first still photograph was taken in 1827 and the first "illusion toys" were invented in the early 1830s—devices that gave the appearance of moving pictures. The world of illusion is Neptunian and, maybe for this reason, its nature is elusive and difficult to define. Neptune's discovery also coincided with advancement in the world of pharmaceuticals. In September 1846 ether was used for the first time, marking a new era in surgery, and in the following year chloroform was first used. Also, the word "anesthetic," derived from the Greek word for "insensible," came into use. Gas began to replace oil for lighting, and street lights opened up a whole new night world, with brightly lit bars offering a seductive, alcoholic retreat.

WORLD OF ESCAPISM

In these ways, Neptune has come to speak of escapism in all its guises. Whether it's the glamor of the movies or the hazy world of drugs and drink, the Neptunian world is cut off from reality or anesthetized from pain. Saturn restricts, Uranus explodes, but Neptune dissolves, into the ether or down the neck of a bottle.

However, to seek existence in such a world is illusory. The movie finishes, the drugs wear off, the hangover brings sickness, and suffering is even more acute. Thus, the two sides to Neptune are rapture or despair, delirious happiness versus pain and confusion. Life is either full of meaning and euphoria or it is pointless. Neptunian types are highly sensitive to either state and must learn that Venus rules true love whereas Neptune rules the fantasy of ideal love and the quest for romance that may or may not be satisfied.

In Greek mythology Neptune is Poseidon, god of the sea, as illustrated in Neptune's glyph of the trident. Thus Neptune rules the ocean and all that is related to it, such as sailing, boats, fishing, and marine life. In the Neptunian world we can be "all at sea" with no land in sight—drifting and floundering—and typical Neptune types know no boundaries. In this respect, Neptune shares many typical Piscean characteristics.

Pluto

SIGN OF DIGNITY SCORPIO

COLOR BLACK

DAY OF THE WEEK NONE

METAL PLUTONIUM

Co-ruler of Scorpio, whose traditional ruler is Mars, Pluto takes approximately 248 years to make its circuit of the zodiac. Pluto was discovered in 1930, comparatively recently in terms of astrological recognition. The most notable event of this era was the development of nuclear power. Thus Pluto has come to signify enormous power that can release untold energy, destroy, or annihilate.

In Greek mythology Pluto is Hades, god of the underworld, and the era of Pluto, including both Nazism and the use of nuclear bombs, certainly presents an unparalleled vision of hell. At its worst, Pluto symbolizes the abuse of power, hellish experiences, and the threat of death, either physically or to a sense of self. In mythology we learn that Hades donned the helmet of invisibility when leaving the underworld. Thus Pluto also speaks of that which is invisible or absent.

The era of Pluto's discovery saw huge advancement in psychotherapy. Entering into therapy constitutes the exploration of our underworld, unearthing our hidden issues, which, in the light of day, can heal us.

TRANSFORMATION

But Pluto's domain is not simply fear, loss, or nothingness. Its depths hold a fascination for us, and when we look more deeply, we find that, with power in the right hands, Pluto stands for awesome achievement and the ability to transform. Note, however, that Plutonic transformation can be a long and painful process, not the wave of a magic wand. Many Plutonic or Scorpionic types achieve, or are born into, positions of great status that require enormous powers of endurance, acting as key figures in the development and growth of society.

Pluto can also signify riches, as its name is derived from "plutos," the Greek word for wealth. Scorpio Bill Gates has Pluto in bold Leo, next to Jupiter—an increasing force—in the money sector of his chart.

STRENGTHS AND WEAKNESSES

Learning about the signs and planets are the first two rungs on the astrological ladder. Once we have grasped their main symbolic purpose and message we can get creative, combining different signs with different planets. The many different combinations will offer their own possible meanings, but an important starting point is to know where traditional astrology assigns strength or weakness.

Degrees of exaltation

SUN
19 degrees
Aries

MOON
3 degrees
Taurus

MERCURY
15 degrees
Virgo

VENUS
27 degrees
Pisces

MARS
28 degrees
Capricorn

JUPITER
15 degrees
Cancer

SATURN
21 degrees
Libra

Astrology is full of symmetry, as has already been illustrated with the allocation of elements and modes, and in the following pages you will find that there is a definite pattern and logical sequence in the distribution of planetary power. The descriptions offered here are not definitive but are designed to demonstrate how the combination of planets and signs can speak of a whole range of matters, all different yet all in keeping with their own domains. It is essential that symbolism is allowed to remain fluid and playful rather than being boxed up and categorized.

DIGNITY, DETRIMENT, EXALTATION, AND FALL

A planet is said to be in dignity or strongly placed, when it is in the sign or signs that it rules, as explored in the first section of this chapter. This is when a planet is "at home," so to speak, as there is a sympathy between the planet and its own sign. For example, we can see that the blaze of the Sun is perfectly at home in fixed and fiery Leo, creating a sense of synergy and symbolic appositeness.

The opposite principle also applies, as when a planet is in the opposite sign to its sign of dignity it is said to be in detriment or debilitated—weakly placed. There is little or no sympathy between the planet and the sign, resulting in friction or a conflict of some kind, which creates a symbolic discord.

In addition to signs of dignity and detriment, the first seven planets—the personal planets—also have a sign of exaltation, the sign in which the qualities of that planet are especially powerful. These placings are also assigned a particular degree for their ultimate position of exaltation. The Sun, for example, is exalted in any degree of Aries but its strongest placing is at 19 degrees.

Again, the opposite principle applies. When a planet is in the opposite sign to its sign of exaltation it is said to be in fall, at its least potent or troublesome in some way. A planet's most difficult placing would, then, be opposite its degree of exaltation, for example, the Moon at 3 degrees of Scorpio.

A planet's symbolic power is also said to be weakened if it is retrograde—backtracking through a sign instead of moving forward. This applies particularly to Mercury, Venus, and Mars.

In the following pages I will look at the placings of detriment, exaltation, and fall for each planet. As the positions of dignity are discussed earlier in the chapter, I will not repeat them here.

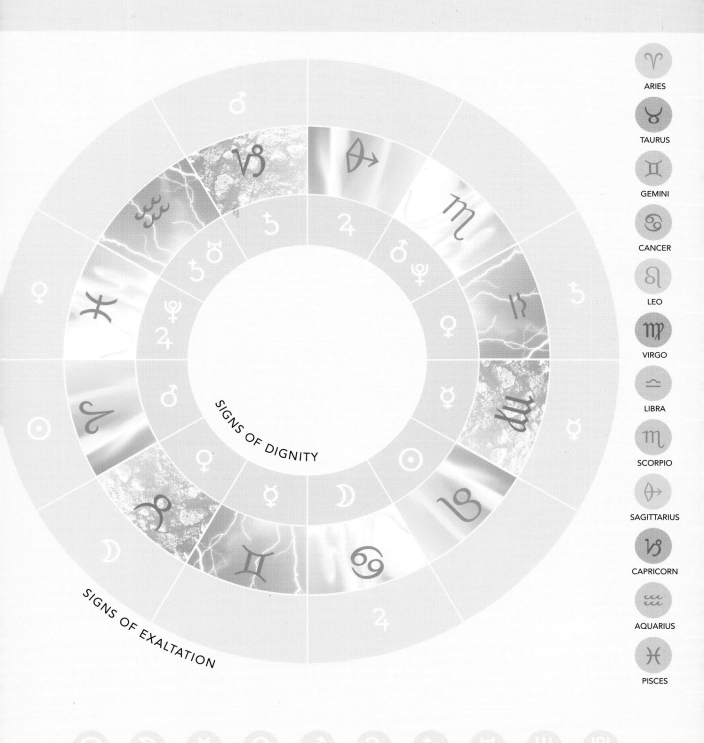

SIGNS OF DIGNITY

SIGNS OF EXALTATION

ARIES
TAURUS
GEMINI
CANCER
LEO
VIRGO
LIBRA
SCORPIO
SAGITTARIUS
CAPRICORN
AQUARIUS
PISCES

SUN MOON MERCURY VENUS MARS JUPITER SATURN URANUS NEPTUNE PLUTO

THE SUN

SIGN OF DETRIMENT
Aquarius, ruled by Saturn

The Sun and Saturn are always enemies, being weak in each other's signs. Aquarius is cool, detached, and objective, and these are Saturnian qualities rather than solar. The Sun cannot shine in Aquarius. Logic presides over heat or passion.

SIGN OF EXALTATION
Aries, ruled by Mars

The Sun and Mars are allies, both being masculine and associated with drive and energy. Both the Sun and Aries are connected with the element of fire and the sense of self. The Sun blazes in this sign.

SIGN OF FALL
Libra, ruled by Venus

Libra is known for deliberation, prevarication, and partnership. A sense of self can be overshadowed by the awareness or need of others. Uncertainty, guilt, or the desire to please presides over egoism.

COMBUST, UNDER SUNBEAMS, AND CAZIMI PLANETS

If another planet is conjunct—placed next to—the Sun to within seven and a half degrees, and in the same sign, then that other planet is said to be combust. This means that it is weakened by its closeness to the Sun, whose powerful rays can burn and overwhelm. For example, the Sun at 10 degrees of Aries, conjunct Mercury at 15 degrees of Aries, places Mercury conjunct the Sun by 5 degrees and it therefore becomes combust.

Any planet within 17 degrees of the Sun is said to be under sunbeams and is weakened, but far less than a combust planet. The Sun at 10 degrees of Aries and Mercury at 25 degrees of Aries places Mercury 15 degrees away from the Sun, and Mercury is therefore under sunbeams.

If a planet conjuncts the Sun to within 17 minutes, it is said to be cazimi. In this position the other planet becomes extremely powerful by being in the heart of the Sun, drawing upon the solar strength and energy. For example, the Sun at 10 degrees and 30 minutes of Aries, and Mercury at 10 degrees and 20 minutes of Aries, places Mercury within 10 minutes of the Sun and it is therefore cazimi.

THE MOON

SIGN OF DETRIMENT
Capricorn, ruled by Saturn

As with the Sun, the Moon and Saturn are enemies, as they are weak in each other's signs. Capricorn is known for austerity, ambition, and achievement in the world. This is in conflict with the Moon's role, which is to nourish, protect, and harbor. The Moon in Capricorn may be infertility, duty before pleasure, over-controlled feelings, or difficulty with empathy.

SIGN OF EXALTATION
Taurus, ruled by Venus

The Moon and Venus are allies, as they are both feminine. The Moon flourishes in fertile Taurus and may symbolize the "earth mother" type, green fingers, enjoying the sensual pleasures of life, or—with Taurus' connection to the throat—a beautiful voice.

SIGN OF FALL
Scorpio, ruled by Mars

The Moon and Mars are enemies and make for a very painful combination. The emotional intensity and sexual power of Mars and Scorpio are in conflict with the soft and receptive lunar qualities. The Moon in Scorpio may be emotional trauma, gynecological problems, or jealousy—but it is often a powerful placing for healing, therapy, or psychic abilities.

The Moon in fertile Taurus can represent an "earth mother" type of person.

 MERCURY

SIGNS OF DETRIMENT
Sagittarius and Pisces, ruled by Jupiter

Mercury is the voice, the mind, and the messenger, at home with the clever tongue of Gemini and the precision of Virgo. Mercury in the Jupiter-ruled signs is less disciplined or controlled.
Mercury in Sagittarius can be tactless, a chatterbox, prone to exaggeration, or going off at tangents. It is a positive placing for learning, prolific writing, wide interests, and liberal attitudes. Often there is a love of debate and satirical wit.
Mercury in Pisces can be unfocused, imprecise, or given to deception, either deliberate lying or being imaginative with the truth. This combination is often a positive placing for acting, writing, or singing.

SIGN OF EXALTATION
Virgo, ruled by Mercury

Mercury is the only planet whose sign of exaltation is the same as one of its signs of dignity. The Mercurial dexterity, accuracy, and communicative skills are perfectly manifested in the sign of mutable earth.

SIGN OF FALL
Pisces, ruled by Jupiter

See Pisces as a sign of detriment for Mercury (above).

 VENUS

SIGNS OF DETRIMENT
Aries and Scorpio, ruled by Mars

Venus and Mars symbolize the polarity of feminine and masculine and they are badly placed in each other's signs. Signs ruled by Mars speak of egoism, drive, force, energy, and power, conflicting with the

slowness, softness, and sensual qualities of the
Venusian nature.

Venus in Aries can be insecure and needy, often
resulting from a difficult adolescence. The hunger for
love makes Venus in Aries the loved rather than the
lover. Venus in Aries may accept love from anyone
rather than a special someone.

Venus in Scorpio is a "femme fatale" or a lover of
sexually attractive and powerful women. Venus in
Scorpio can speak of power issues in love, struggles
with jealousy, a need for revenge when love goes
wrong, and anger toward feminine power.

SIGN OF EXALTATION
Pisces, ruled by Jupiter

The nature of Venus is magnified through sensitive
and imaginative Pisces. The flow of boundless love
recognizes no boundaries. Venus in Pisces can be
associated with women, beauty, and people who are
affectionate or vulnerable, often artistic or musical,
and also lovers of the arts.

SIGN OF FALL
Virgo, ruled by Mercury

Virgo seeks perfection, so little wonder that this is
Venus' sign of fall—love is rarely perfect. This
combination can be over-discriminating, easily
disappointed, the celibate, or a "not-a-hair-out-of-
place," beautiful type of person.

 MARS

SIGNS OF DETRIMENT
Taurus and Libra, ruled by Venus

The nature of Venus is always to relate, negotiate, and
cooperate, conflicting with the single-minded nature
of Mars, whose purpose is to move forward, either to
achieve or attack.

Mars in Taurus is a difficult combination. The planet
of action in the sign of fixed earth can be stuck or
lacking motivation. At worst it is bullying. It can also
speak of the abuser or the abused, staying power, and
hands-on work such as gardening.

Mars in Libra also symbolizes a conflict of energies,
with Mars trying to find a way forward in the sign of
the scales—direct action versus balance, and personal
agendas under the guise of diplomacy. It can suggest
fighting for peace and passive-aggressive behavior.

SIGN OF EXALTATION
Capricorn, ruled by Saturn

The drive and energy of Mars is honed and harnessed
in the sign of cardinal earth. Mars in Capricorn can
speak of action with a purpose, the successful
executive, and the hard worker. In physical terms, this
combination is strong and wiry.

*Venus in Pisces can suggest
artistic or musical people.*

SIGN OF FALL
Cancer, ruled by the Moon

Mars in the Moon's sign of dignity is a painful mismatch. It suggests being easily hurt, a lack of, or aggressive, parenting, feeling fearful, and having stomach disorders.

2♃ JUPITER

SIGNS OF DETRIMENT
Gemini and Virgo, ruled by Mercury

Jupiter and Mercury, as already discussed, represent opposite principles. They are therefore ill-placed in each other's signs.

Jupiter in Gemini may signify a conflict between right and wrong and theory and practice, with Jupiter representing the higher mind, and Mercury the lower. This combination can speak of questions of faith, too many choices, being playful, having a big imagination, and wanting two or more of everything.

Jupiter in Virgo can make a mountain out of a molehill, with expansive Jupiter in the sign of detail and discrimination. This combination suggests too much work and an obsessive-compulsive person. It can be a positive placing for ethical values, health workers, and allegiance to others.

SIGN OF EXALTATION
Cancer, ruled by the Moon

Jupiter and the Moon are allies as neither is troubled in the other's sign(s). Jupiter's benefic but often boundless qualities are perfectly contained in Cancer, the sign of nurture. This combination may suggest the rescuer and protector, and mother love.

Mars in Capricorn can symbolize the successful executive and hard work.

SIGN OF FALL
Capricorn, ruled by Saturn

Expansive Jupiter in the sign of restraint can speak of pleasure versus duty and freedom versus discipline. It suggests rules imposed "for your own good," hard work, disapproval of waste, and the ambassador for foreign affairs or human rights.

♄ SATURN

SIGNS OF DETRIMENT
Cancer and Leo, ruled by the Moon and the Sun respectively (the Lights and Saturn are enemies)

With the slower moving planets it is important to remember that their journeys through a particular sign will be carried by a whole generation. For example, Saturn was in Cancer and Leo through 1914–18 (the First World War), and again in Cancer from June 1944–August 1946, marking the end of the Second World War and all of those born into the hardship of its aftermath.

Saturn in Cancer is a difficult placing. Saturn is ill at ease in the Moon's sign. This combination can speak of an unhappy start in life, heavy-handed parenting, introversion, and homelessness.

Saturn in Leo is an obvious mismatch. Saturn is cold, the Sun is hot, so Saturn in the Sun's sign is a misplacing. It is connected with denial of self-expression and personal fulfillment coming later in life. The need to assert the ego can create disciplinarian attitudes and imposition of the will without empathy.

SIGN OF EXALTATION
Libra, ruled by Venus

Serious Saturn is mellowed and equalized in Venus' masculine sign. It suggests authority at its best—the benevolent father, the wise judge, and also with the beauty of structure and symmetry.

SIGN OF FALL
Aries, ruled by Mars

The sign of action and ego slams its head against Saturn's brick walls. This combination can speak of innovation versus tradition, resentment of authority, but with personal discipline as a saving grace, and with headaches and migraines.

THE OUTER PLANETS

Uranus, Neptune and Pluto are the three "modern" planets, so called because they were unknown to ancient astronomy. They are commonly known as the Transaturnians—the planets that come after Saturn—or as the non-personal planets, as each is a co-ruler of a particular sign and not a substitute for the traditional ruler. Their main importance lies in the aspects they make in the horoscope to the personal planets, and their activity by transit or progression, which will be covered in chapters five and six.

These last three planets move slowly and are generational. From September 1957–September 1961, Uranus was in Leo, Neptune in Scorpio, and Pluto in Virgo, so everyone born in this period has these planets in these signs. They are less important in terms of personal characteristics but can add meaning if they are linked with the personal planets.

URANUS THE CO-RULER OF AQUARIUS	NEPTUNE THE CO-RULER OF PISCES	PLUTO THE CO-RULER OF SCORPIO
Sign of Detriment LEO	Sign of Detriment VIRGO	Sign of Detriment TAURUS
Uranus is connected with society, the good of the whole, technology, machinery that does the work of a hundred people, and all that is impersonal and objective. Uranus is in conflict with Leo, the sign of individual creativity and artistry.	*Neptune is associated with boundlessness, the world of feelings, escapism, going with the flow, dreams and fantasies, confusion, or glamor. Neptune is in conflict with Virgo, the sign of work and service, order, and minimalism.*	*Pluto speaks of the unconscious, the polarity of destruction and healing, death and rebirth, and all that is hidden, dangerous, or mysterious. Pluto is in conflict with Taurus, the sign of physical safety, home comforts, and all that is visible and tangible.*

Traditional astrology does not recognize or posit signs of exaltation and fall for the outer planets. For details of their signs of detriment, see the box on page 48.

CHIRON

Most modern ephemerides now list the position of Chiron. This planet was discovered on 1 November 1977 and, in spite of its relative modernity, is fast gaining astrological credibility. Its orbit is approximately 50 years and modern astrology has postulated that it is the co-ruler of Sagittarius.

WHAT DOES CHIRON SYMBOLIZE?
In mythology Chiron was a centaur, half man and half horse, and the son of Saturn. However, he was raised by Apollo, who taught Chiron the skills of both warfare and healing. He was also granted the gift of immortality, which became his curse as, once wounded with poison, he could neither heal himself nor die. His redemption lay in relinquishing his immortality. Chiron thus symbolizes where we are wounded, and can speak of karmic pain that the soul carries forward and which has yet to be released and transformed in the current life. Whether or not you accept the idea of past lives and karma, astrology indicates that the nature of Chiron is akin to that of Pluto, who also demands that we transform and strengthen our lives through experiences of loss or suffering.

RETROGRADE PLANETS
Planets do not literally stop and turn around, but a retrograde planet is one that, from our viewpoint on Earth, appears to be moving backward rather than forward. Apart from the Sun and the Moon, all the planets spend periods of time in retrograde motion. The further away from the Sun, the longer the period of retrograde motion, so for this reason the swiftest moving bodies of Mercury, Venus, and Mars are the most important in terms of personal meaning.

The initial "R" in the ephemerides tells you the day that a planet turns retrograde and the initial "D" tells you when it resumes direct motion (see page 156.) The degree and minute at which a planet turns retrograde or direct is called its "station."

THE SYMBOLISM OF RETROGRADE PLANETS
Retrograde signifies that a planet's positive qualities are reversed, withheld, or delayed in some way. When the personal planets go through their retrograde periods they usually signify a theme of slowing down and having to rethink life.

RETROGRADE MERCURY
Mercury turns retrograde three or four times a year, for about three weeks at a time. During these periods life is notoriously chaotic, as retrograde Mercury plays havoc

Chiron, the mythological immortal centaur, symbolizes karmic pain.

with communication, transport, and information of all kinds. Often there is a theme of one step forward, two steps back, plans unraveling, back to the drawing board, and so on. When Mercury turns direct the truth comes out, details come to light, we are ready to talk, or we change our minds. It is unwise to make decisions until Mercury goes direct. Also, retrograde Mercury often signifies getting back in touch with someone important.

In a horoscope a retrograde Mercury can signify delays or problems in early education, learning how to speak out, difficulty with articulating thoughts or feelings to others, a speech impediment, or reticence.

RETROGRADE MARS

Mars turns retrograde approximately every 25 months for periods of around 65–80 days. This can put the brakes on enterprises requiring initiative or force, or it can spell ill-advised action that may be regretted, delaying tactics, or a repression of desire or of the will.

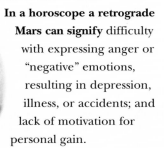

In a horoscope a retrograde Mars can signify difficulty with expressing anger or "negative" emotions, resulting in depression, illness, or accidents; and lack of motivation for personal gain.

RETROGRADE VENUS

Venus turns retrograde once every 18–20 months and stays retrograde for around 42 days. Affairs of the heart are especially delicate, misleading, or difficult to resolve at these times. Relationships started under a retrograde Venus may not last, but rifts and splits can be mended when it goes direct. Apart from the obvious emotional concerns, a retrograde Venus can speak of day-to-day disappointments, such as lost valuable items and damaged goods.

In a horoscope a retrograde Venus can signify difficulty with expressing love or feelings, shyness, inability to commit, or marrying late in life.

THE PART OF FORTUNE

There are several components in a horoscope that are not "real" in the sense that the planets are real. The Ascendant, for example, is the main angle of the horoscope, which locates the rising sign and can be found only through mathematical calculation. The same applies to the Part of Fortune, as this is an imaginary point, derived from the formula of the Ascendant, plus the Moon, minus the Sun (see page 61). The Part of Fortune picks out a lucky point. However, it is rare for a single feature to carry great importance in its own right and this is true both of the Part of Fortune and the Moon's nodes. Both of these features are at their most powerful when conjunct—next to—another planet or an angle, drawing attention to that planet or angle, for good or ill.

THE MOON'S NODES

You will find the position of the Moon's nodes in their own column in the ephemerides (see page 156), listed as "Mean"—averaged-out movement—or "True"—their exact movement.

The North Node This marks where the Moon crosses the ecliptic from south to north.

The South Node This marks where the Moon crosses the ecliptic from north to south.

WHAT ARE THE MOON'S NODES?

Every horoscope will show the position of the nodes by their glyphs, but they are in fact imaginary points at which the Moon cuts across the ecliptic—the celestial sphere that marks the apparent orbit of the Sun. The ecliptic takes its name from the fact that eclipses can happen only when the Moon is on or near this line. The nodes are always exactly opposite each other. You will find only the north node listed in the ephemerides, as the south node is opposite.

In traditional astrology the line of the nodes symbolizes a dragon, with the north node known as Caput Draconis—the head of the dragon, and the south node known as Cauda Draconis—the tail of the dragon. The Sun and the Moon are considered as the eyes of the dragon, and the dragon "eating" the Lights refers to the phenomenon of eclipses.

The north node is regarded as fortunate, as this is where the dragon feeds and gains nourishment. The south node is regarded as unfortunate, being where the dragon excretes. Another suggestion is that the north node signifies good karma and the south node shows bad karma.

FIXED STARS

Fixed stars move through the zodiac at a rate of 50 seconds of arc a year, so they are found at the same degree for around 120 years at a time. Fixed stars do not have the same weight as the planets or angles, do not have glyphs, and are not found in the horoscope. They can act as a '"testimony" to interpretation, but are only considered to be prominent if they are conjunct a planet or angle to within one degree. For example, the Sun at 29 degrees of Leo is dignified by being in its own sign, but it gathers strength by being conjunct the fixed star of Regulus. Conversely, Mars at 26 degrees of Taurus is troubled by being in its sign of detriment, but is afflicted further by being conjunct the malefic fixed star of Algol.

Many of the fixed stars are assigned quite dramatic meanings in traditional astrology, but in modern-day practice it is important to remember that their value is not to alarm but to assist interpretation. No client would wish to hear, for instance, that a planet in his or her chart is conjunct a star of violent death or suicide. This information can be fascinating to the astrologer but needs to be used with great care in practice.

The box below does not show a complete list but comprises of the major benefic and malefic fixed stars.

MALEFIC FIXED STARS

Alcyone 29 Taurus. "The Weeping Sisters." Denotes sorrow and tears.

Aldebaran 9 Gemini. Honor, courage, intelligence, energy, risk of violence or sickness.

Algol 26 Taurus. Risk of violence or physical danger.

Antares 9 Sagittarius. Warlike, self-destructive, blindness.

Scheat 29 Pisces. Sadness, cruelty, misfortune, imprisonment, death or suicide, especially by drowning.

Serpentis 19 Scorpio. "The accursed degree of the accursed sign," considered as the most malefic degree of the zodiac.

Vindemiatrix 9 Libra. The star of widowhood, loss, or disgrace.

BENEFIC FIXED STARS

North Scale 19 Scorpio. High intelligence, riches, and happiness.

Regulus 29 Leo. Ambition, honor, success, and leadership.

Spica 23 Libra. One of the most fortunate stars, denoting fertility and success.

Vega (or Wega) 15 Capricorn. Fortunate, refined, skill in politics.

A horoscope is a map of the heavens as seen from the place of birth and at the time of birth. The quadrants of the horoscope create the all-important angles—including the Ascendant—and the division of the horoscope into 12 segments creates the houses. As with the signs and the planets, each house has its own dominion. The positioning of the planets in the houses adds another layer of meaning and reveals the aspects between one planet and another. Assessing the combinations of planets, signs, houses, and aspects plays a vital role in bringing a horoscope to life.

3

THE HOROSCOPE

CHART CALCULATION

If the thought of casting a horoscope strikes terror into your heart then you are not alone. Quite often those who are mathematically inclined are to be found in the scientific world, while those of a philosophical or artistic bent are more likely to be drawn toward such subjects as astrology. It follows, therefore, that many astrologers are not natural mathematicians and I used to consider myself as positively innumerate.

The advent of computer packages for chart calculation has eradicated the need for working figures out longhand, and it could be said that this is a dying skill. You can now tap the data into a computer and the angles and planets are worked out in seconds. So why bother learning how to calculate a chart by hand?

One reason is that not all of us have access to a computer, but the real value in learning chart calculation is that it brings you much closer to the intricate workings of astrology. You need not always calculate by hand, but there is no substitute for familiarizing yourself with the technique when it comes to understanding the motion of the planets. This knowledge will also assist your understanding of transits and progressions—the timing measures that are required for predictive work.

STEP BY STEP, HOW TO CALCULATE A HOROSCOPE

There are many different house systems but it is not within the scope of this book to examine and compare them. The horoscopes in this book are all calculated using Placidus, as this is the system most commonly used, using Raphael's Tables of Houses for Northern Latitudes.
Example:
Catherine Zeta-Jones
25 September 1969
14.40 BST
Swansea—51N37, 3W57

1 GMT TIME OF BIRTH
Always work with Greenwich Mean Time (GMT). In this example the birthtime is BST—British Summer Time—so the time of birth in GMT is one hour earlier—13.40 GMT.

2 SIDEREAL TIME
In the ephemerides you will see that the first column is called S.T. (Sidereal Time)—"star" time. This is listed in h-m-s (hours, minutes, and seconds). Don't confuse this with the planets, which are listed as degrees, minutes, and sometimes seconds— there being 60 seconds to 1 minute, 60 minutes to 1 degree, and 30 degrees to each sign. Round this figure up or down to the nearest minute. In this example the S.T. is 00h 14m 33s and this is rounded up to 00.15.

3 ACCELERATION
For every complete 6 hours of time that has elapsed between midnight and the time of birth we have to add 1 minute of sidereal time. Hence, with our example of a birth time of 13.40, two complete 6-hour periods have elapsed so we therefore add 2 minutes.

4 GST
Add the S.T. and the GMT time of birth and the acceleration—00.15 + 13.40 + 00.02 = 13.57. This gives the GST—Greenwich Sidereal Time.

Also, a computer is only as accurate as the data you put in so, if you know how a chart hangs together, you will quickly spot any mistakes made when using software. To calculate a horoscope, you need: ephemerides, house tables, a calculator.

EPHEMERIDES

As explained in chapter one ephemerides are the tables that list the daily motions of the planets, telling us which sign they are in and how fast they are moving. You can purchase ephemerides (and house tables) in many "new age" shops. There are ephemerides available that list the planets for midnight (0h) or midday (12h). I recommend that you use midnight

ephemerides so that you are always working within one day, rather than a 24-hour period divided between two days. This chapter consistently uses midnight ephemerides.

WHAT IS A HOROSCOPE?

Your horoscope is like a photograph of the heavens, as if someone had looked up at your place and time of birth and taken a picture. In this sense it is frozen in time, capturing the astronomical image of the birth moment. In order to reproduce that image astrologically by calculating a horoscope, the first thing you

1 Cusp of 1st house

FIRST HOUSE

2 Cusp of 2nd house

SECOND HOUSE

3 Cusp of 3rd house

THIRD HOUSE

4 Cusp of 4th house

The cusps mark the beginning of each house and are marked to the degree.

5 LONGITUDE CORRECTION
Remember that we have standardized time and the whole world is divided into convenient time zones—but imagine if you were telling the time using a sundial? The angle of the sundial's shadow as seen in London would be different from the angle of the shadow as seen in Edinburgh. The same time zone is not equivalent to the same clocktime so the astrologer makes allowance for this difference by calculating a longitude correction.

Formula: Multiply the longitude by 4. In this example, 3W57 x 4 = 15.48. We arrive at this figure by multiplying the degrees of longitude first (3 x 4 = 12) and then the minutes of longitude (57 x 4 = 228 or 3.8 degrees). Convert 3.8 degrees into degrees and minutes of longitude by multiplying 0.8 by 0.60 (0.8 x 0.60 = 0.48), giving 3.48. Add 12 and 3.48 together (12 + 3.48 = 15.48). Then round this up or down to the nearest degree. The longitude correction in this example is 16.

6 LST
If the longitude of the place of birth is west then subtract the longitude correction. If the longitude of the place of birth is east, then add the longitude correction. In this example we must subtract 16 from the GST as the place of birth is west, so 13.57 – 16 = 13.41. This final figure

is the LST—Local Sidereal Time. (n.b. The final figure must be under 24.00. If it is over then simply subtract 24.00 to give the LST.) See the chart below for a summary of how to calculate the Local Sidereal Time.

TIME OF BIRTH	14.40 BST
CORRECTION TO GMT	– 1 HOUR 13.40 GMT
S.T.—SIDEREAL TIME AT 0H	00.15
ACCELERATION	00.02
ADDED TOGETHER TO GIVE GST	= 13.57
LONGITUDE CORRECTION (WEST/SUBTRACT—EAST/ADD)	00.16
FINAL ANSWER—LST	13.41

need to know is the exact location of the planets in the sky. The planets then need to be placed on the horoscopic wheel to show the position on earth from which the picture has been taken. For every horoscope you will need:

Date of birth

Time of birth—accurate as possible

Place of birth—the latitude and longitude

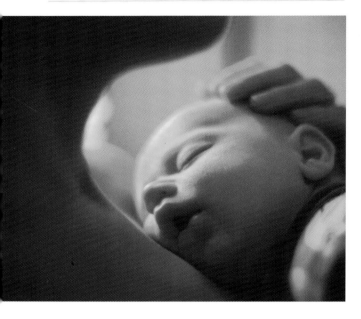

These are always written as degrees and minutes with N or S to indicate North or South latitude, and W or E to indicate West or East longitude. For example, Manchester 53N30, 2W15; Athens 37N58, 23E43; New York 40N45, 73W57; Sydney 33S52, 151E13.

CALCULATING THE ANGLES

The horoscopic wheel is divided into four quadrants to give the angles of the chart—the main axes—and each quadrant is divided into three to give the 12 houses, or divisions, of the horoscope. First, you need to find out which sign is on which cusp (the beginning of each house), and at what degree.

HOUSE TABLES

You now have the information needed to determine the house cusps. Turn to your house tables and find the place that corresponds most closely with the latitude of birth. In the example below, Swansea is at 51N37, corresponding most closely with the house tables for London at 51N32.

Again, the first column is sidereal time, listed in hours, minutes, and seconds, and each line is about 4 minutes apart. In this column look for the closest sidereal time—or h m s—to your final LST answer of 13.41. In the example below, the nearest sidereal time is 13.40.12.

The signs appear at the top of each column, and a change of sign—moving from 30 degrees of one sign to 0 degrees of the next—is indicated by the glyph for the next sign in the column. You can now read off the degrees for the house cusps. We are looking for the house cusps for 13.41, so the line for 13.40.12 is close enough to be almost exact. If you want to be even more accurate you can add roughly a quarter of the difference between lines 2 and 3. Computer software does this automatically but this level of accuracy is not really necessary, especially as most birth times are approximate. As a rule of thumb, round up the tenth house cusp (also known as the Midheaven) and the first house cusp (known as the Ascendant) to the nearest quarter degree and all the other house cusps to the nearest full degree.

SIDEREAL TIME			10 ♎	11 ♏	12 ♐	ASCEN ♐		2 ♒	3 ♓
H.	M.	S.	°	°	°	°	'	°	°
13	36	25	26	19	7	22	06	5	22
13	40	12	27	20	7	22	54	6	23
13	44	00	28	21	8	23	42	7	25

Example of House Tables for London at 51N32

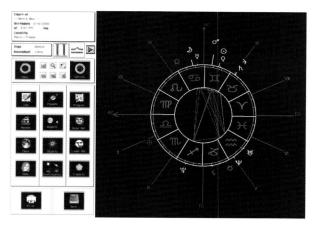

Computer software can calculate birth charts in seconds.

The cusps for Catherine Zeta-Jones' chart are:

10th—27 and a quarter Libra

11th—20 Scorpio

12th—7 Sagittarius

Asc—23 Sagittarius

2nd—6 Aquarius

3rd—23 Pisces

THE OTHER HOUSE CUSPS

The framework of a horoscope is completely symmetrical so the other house cusps are found simply by keeping the same degree but substituting the opposite signs. For this example:

4th—27 and a quarter Aries

5th—20 Taurus

6th—7 Gemini

Desc—23 Gemini

8th—6 Leo

9th—23 Virgo

INTERCEPTED HOUSES

You will notice in Catherine Zeta-Jones' chart that two signs are duplicated—Sagittarius is on the first house cusp (the Ascendant) and also on the 12th. Therefore the opposite sign of Gemini is to be found on the seventh house cusp (the Descendant) and also on the sixth. This means that two signs are missing and have to be slotted in.

In this example, Capricorn and Cancer are the two missing signs. Capricorn takes its place between Sagittarius and Aquarius and is therefore intercepted in the first house. Cancer takes its place between Gemini and Leo and is therefore intercepted in the seventh house.

SIZE OF THE HOUSES

You will notice that the horoscopic wheel is divided equally into 12 sections—the houses—but in reality all the houses are of different sizes. For example, the first house covers the area from 23 degrees of Sagittarius to 6 degrees of Aquarius—comprising of 43 degrees in all; the second house covers the area from 6 degrees of Aquarius to 23 degrees of Pisces—47 degrees; the third house covers the area from 23 degrees of Pisces to 27 and a quarter degrees of Aries—34 and a quarter degrees, and so on.

Some horoscopes mark 360 degrees on the outside of the wheel and the houses are divided up to show their exact size in relation to each other. However, I have never found the size of the house to be important in interpretation. I feel that a symbolic representation of the horoscope—dividing it into 12 equal sections—is a more user-friendly format.

CALCULATING THE PLANETS

Having calculated the house cusps—the framework of the chart—the astrologer's next task is to calculate the exact position of the planets and then place them in the correct houses.

On any given date the ephemerides will list the position of the planets for exactly midnight. Unless someone happens to be born at exactly midnight you will have to make an adjustment for the time of birth. For example, for someone born at 6.00am you would have to calculate how far the planets had moved in the six hours from their midnight position to 6.00am. Here is a quick and easy method for finding the planetary positions that does not involve the use of logarithms and can be done with a calculator.

CONVERT THE BIRTH TIME INTO MINUTES

Again, always work with the time of birth in GMT. Catherine Zeta-Jones was born at 14.40 BST—so 13.40 GMT. 13h 40m converts to 820 minutes.

DAILY MOTION

Now note the position of the planets at midnight on the day of birth and at midnight on the next day so that you can find the Daily Motion—how far the planet has moved within that 24-hour period. For example, at 0h (midnight) 25 September 1969 the Sun is at 1 degree and 45 minutes of Libra. At 0h 26 September 1969 the Sun is at 2 degrees and 44 minutes of Libra. The Sun's daily motion is therefore 59 minutes. (This is commonly referred to as 59 minutes of arc.)

THE FORMULA

This is the birth time in minutes, divided by the total number of minutes in a day (1440), multiplied by the Daily Motion. So, 820 divided by 1440, multiplied by 59 = 34 minutes of arc.

FINAL ANSWER

Add your answer to the first midnight position of the Sun—1 degree and 45 minutes of Libra—and this will tell you how far the Sun has traveled, giving the exact position of the Sun at the time of birth—2 degrees and 19 minutes of Libra.

This is always written as the planet's glyph, followed by the degree, glyph for the sign, and then the minutes. So ☉2≏19. Now apply exactly the same method to the rest of the planets and the Moon's nodes if you are using True nodes as opposed to Mean (averaged-out position).

THE MOON

Notice how swiftly the Moon moves in comparison to the other planets. It changes sign approximately every two-and-a-half days.

- At 0h 25 September 1969 the Moon is at 20 degrees and 38 minutes of Pisces.
- At 0h 26 September 1969 the Moon is at 4 degrees and 42 minutes of Aries.
- The Moon's daily motion is therefore 14 degrees and 04 minutes, or 844 minutes of arc.

- Formula—820 divided by 1440, multiplied by 844 = 481, or 8 degrees and 1 minute.
- Add this figure to your first 0h position for the Moon and you have ☽28♓39. (As the Moon is so fast-moving you may sometimes find a difference of a minute of arc or two between hand-calculated or computer-calculated positions. Such tiny differences are unimportant.)

MERCURY

Mercury's daily motion varies enormously because of the three or four periods a year in which it is retrograde. In other words, it is often slowing down—to turn retrograde—or speeding up after having turned direct. At its fastest, Mercury's daily motion is just over 2 degrees. You will notice an "℞" in the Mercury column on the line for 17 September 1969, indicating that Mercury turned retrograde the day before on 16 September 1969, so we know that Mercury is moving relatively slowly.

- At 0h 25 September 1969 Mercury is at 10 degrees and 47 minutes of Libra.
- At 0h 26 September 1969 Mercury is at 9 degrees and 47 minutes of Libra, moving backward (because Mercury has turned retrograde).
- Mercury's daily motion is therefore 1 degree, or 60 minutes of arc.
- Formula – 820 divided by 1440, mulitplied by 60 = 34.
- Because Mercury is retrograde *subtract* 34 from the first 0h position for Mercury and this gives you ☿10≏13. Write "℞" after it on the chart, crossing the right leg of the "℞." If a planet has

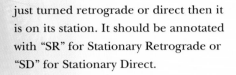

just turned retrograde or direct then it is on its station. It should be annotated with "SR" for Stationary Retrograde or "SD" for Stationary Direct.

VENUS

Venus' daily motion can vary considerably depending on how near it is to retrograde or direct stations. At normal speed Venus' daily motion is just over one degree.

- At 0h 25 September 1969 Venus is at 2 degrees and 15 minutes of Virgo.
- At 0h 26 September 1969 Venus is at 3 degrees and 28 minutes of Virgo.
- Venus' daily motion is therefore 1 degree and 13 minutes, 73 minutes of arc.
- Formula—820 divided by 1440 x by 73 = 42.
- Add this figure to your first 0h position for Venus and this gives you ♀2♍57.

MARS

Unless Mars is turning retrograde or direct its normal daily motion is about 40 minutes of arc, about a third of a degree slower than Venus' normal daily motion. Notice from now on how the planets continue to decrease in speed.

- At 0h 25 September 1969 Mars is at 2 degrees and 19 minutes of Capricorn.
- At 0h 26 September 1969 Mars is at 2 degrees and 57 minutes of Capricorn.
- Mars' daily motion is therefore 38 minutes of arc.
- Formula – 820 divided by 1440 x by 38 = 22.
- Add this figure to your first 0h position for Mars and this gives you ♂2♑41.

JUPITER

Unless Jupiter is turning retrograde or direct its normal daily motion is approximately a quarter of a degree.

- At 0h 25 September 1969 Jupiter is at 13 degrees and 12 minutes of Libra.
- At 0h 26 September 1969 Jupiter is at 13 degrees and 25 minutes of Libra.
- Jupiter's daily motion is therefore 13 minutes of arc.
- Formula—820 divided by 1440, x by 13 = 7.
- Add this figure to your first 0h position for Jupiter and this gives you ♃13♎19.

SATURN

The daily motion of Saturn and the remaining planets is minimal. Unless Saturn is turning retrograde or direct its normal daily motion is only around 6 minutes of arc. Therefore, the position of the last four planets can be calculated without doing sums. In this example note that Saturn is retrograde.

- At 0h 25 September 1969 Saturn is at 7 degrees and 55 minutes of Taurus.
- At 0h 26 September 1969 Saturn is at 7 degrees and 52 minutes of Taurus.
- Saturn's daily motion is therefore just 3 minutes of arc. By midday it will therefore have moved a minute and a half, by 13.40 GMT fractionally further, so you can deduct 2 (i.e. Saturn is retrograde) from the first 0h position for Saturn and this gives you ♄7♉53R.

URANUS

- At 0h 25 September 1969 Uranus is at 4 degrees and 14 minutes of Libra.

- At 0h 26 September 1969 Uranus is at 4 degrees and 18 minutes of Libra.
- Uranus' daily motion is therefore just 4 minutes of arc. For a birth time just after midday you can simply add 2 to the first 0h position for Uranus and this gives you ♅4♎16.

NEPTUNE

- At 0h 25 September 1969 Neptune is at 26 degrees and 33 minutes of Scorpio.
- At 0h 26 September 1969 Neptune is at 26 degrees and 35 minutes of Scorpio.
- Neptune's daily motion is therefore 2 minutes of arc. For a birth time just after midday you can simply add 1 to the first 0h position for Neptune and this gives you ♆26♏34.

PLUTO

- At 0h 25 September 1969 Pluto is at 25 degrees and 11 minutes of Libra.
- At 0h 26 September 1969 Pluto has reached 25 degrees and 14 minutes of Libra.
- Pluto's daily motion is therefore 3 minutes of arc, the same as Saturn's. Just add 2 to the first 0h position for Pluto and this gives you ♇25♏13.

THE MOON'S NODES

The daily motion of the Moon's nodes is very small and can be approximated. In this example, at 0h on both 25 and 26 September the Moon's north node is at 21♓08—so the Moon's south node is at 21♍08.

THE PART OF FORTUNE

This position in the chart is found by the formula of the Ascendant, plus the Moon, minus the Sun. This

can get quite complicated as you are often dealing with figures that add up to more than 30, i.e. more than the number of degrees in one sign, but it is relatively easy to do with practice. Always keep track of the signs by numbering them: Aries 1, Taurus 2, etc.

Example: Catherine Zeta-Jones has the Ascendant at 23♐00, ☽28♓39, and ☉2♎19.

Ascendant at 23.00—in Sagittarius—sign 9
Moon at 28.39—in Pisces—sign 12
= 51.39—in sign 21.

This sum as it stands doesn't make sense, because it is not possible to have 51 degrees of a sign or 21 signs. So, you make an adjustment by subtracting 30 degrees

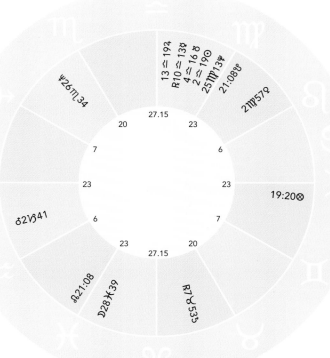

The birth chart for Catherine Zeta-Jones, whose Sun sign is Libra.

(one sign) on the first side, which gives 21.39, and then balance this on the other side by moving one sign forward—sign 22. There are only 12 signs in the zodiac, so you subtract 12 and then you are in sign 10—Capricorn.

Answer 21.39 of Capricorn—sign 10 minus Sun 02.19 of Libra—sign 7 = 19.20 of sign 3 (Gemini), so the Part of Fortune is 19♊20.

I omit the glyphs for the signs when I write the Part of Fortune and the Moon's nodes on the chart as a way of differentiating them from the planets.

PLACING THE PLANETS IN THE HOUSES

Once you have calculated the position of the ten planets, the Moon's nodes, and the Part of Fortune you can then place them on the horoscopic wheel. Remember that you are working anticlockwise. For example, the third house cusp is 23 Pisces so the Moon, at 28♓39, must be placed after the cusp—in the third house. The Moon's north node at 21♓08 is placed just before the cusp to show that the node is conjunct the third cusp. You can see the finished chart on page 61.

If you draw the chart up in your own hand it is good to draw the glyphs and figures as clearly as possible so that they are easily legible.

A HANDY TIP

Think of the wheel of the horoscope as a 24-hour clock—the first house as 6am, the seventh as 6pm, the tenth as midday, and the fourth as midnight. The Sun will indicate the time of birth and can be used as a quick marker of the accuracy of the chart. Catherine Zeta-Jones is born at 13.40 GMT so her Sun must fall in the segment marking 12.00 midday to 14.00—the 9th house. If you find the Sun in the wrong segment then you have done something wrong. This spot-check has saved me from drawing up the wrong chart.

BIRTHS OUTSIDE OF THE UK

The beauty of astrological formulae is that, once you have learned them, you simply apply them over and over again. Calculating a horoscope for a birth outside of the UK follows the same step-by-step procedure. The only thing to look out for is that the GMT time of birth may move the date of birth backward or forward by a day. For example, someone born in Philadelphia at 22.00 on 12 November 1929 would be born at 03.00 GMT on 13 November 1929, so this time and date must be used for all calculations.

Here are the calculations for Grace Kelly whose chart is featured later in this chapter.

Time of birth	05.31
Correction to GMT + 5 hours	10.31
GMT (same day)	
S.T. – Sidereal time at 0h	03.23
Acceleration	00.01
Added together GST	13.55
Longitude correction (West/subtract, East/add)	05.00
Final Answer LST	08.55

12 November 1929
05.31 am (5h west)
Philadelphia, PA
39N57, 75W10

The nearest corresponding house tables are for latitude 39N54. The nearest line is for 8.53.51, which is close enough to read the inner house cusps straight off, but adding another quarter degree to the angles:

10th—11 and a quarter Leo
11th—14 Virgo
12th—12 Libra
Asc—4 and three quarters Scorpio
2nd—3 Sagittarius
3rd—6 Capricorn

Again, the other house cusps are simply the opposite to these and the position of the planets should then be calculated in exactly the same way as demonstrated for Catherine Zeta-Jones, working with the GMT time of birth.

BIRTHS IN SOUTHERN LATITUDES

You will not find house tables for the southern latitudes. This is because you can simply use the house tables for northern latitudes in reverse, just as the signs of long and slow ascension for the northern latitudes are simply inverted for the southern latitudes. The only difference when it comes to the calculations is to factor in an additional 12 hours.

Example: Germaine Greer
29 January 1939
Melbourne, Australia
37S49, 145E00
06.00 (10.00 h East)

Time of birth	*06.00*
Correction to GMT – 10 hours	*20.00*
GMT (previous day)	
S.T. Sidereal time at 0h 28 Jan 39	*08.25*
Acceleration	*00.03*
Added together GST	*= 28.28*
Longitude correction	
(West/subtract, East/add)	*+ 09.40*
LST (then deduct 24 hrs if necessary)	
38.08 – 24 hrs	*= 14.08*
Add 12 hours for southern latitudes	
(then deduct 24 hrs if necessary)	
26.08 – 24 hrs	*= 02.08*
Final answer	*02.08*

HOUSE CUSPS

Melbourne is at 37S49. Now turn to the house tables and find the nearest corresponding tables for northern latitudes, which is Athens at 37N58, and

read off the house cusps. The degrees remain the same but use the opposite signs. A sidereal time of 02.08 gives:

10th—4 and a quarter Taurus → Scorpio

11th—10 Gemini → Sagittarius

12th—14 Cancer → Capricorn

Asc—13 and a quarter Leo →Aquarius

2nd—5 Virgo → Pisces

3rd—2 Libra → Aries

Taking into account tiny adjustments—which occur when rounding up sidereal time or minutes for acceleration—computer software will tell you that Germaine Greer's Midheaven (10th cusp) is 4♏25 and her Ascendant is 13♒16. Again, it is not necessary to be over concerned with these small differences.

PLANETS

Now calculate the position of the planets for the GMT time and date of birth. For Germaine Greer you need to find the position of the planets at 20.00 on the previous day, 28 January 1939.

THE HOUSES

The wheel of the horoscope is divided into 12 houses, or sections, one for each sign. As with the signs and planets, each house has its own dominion, whether this is other people in our lives, work matters, health issues, money, and so on. The concerns of each house are in keeping with the symbolism of the sign and planet(s) to which they correspond. The houses are numbered anti-clockwise.

Angular houses 1,4,7, and 10—so-called because these houses mark the angles—the main axes of the horoscope. They correspond to the cardinal signs. Planets in these houses are at their most visible, active, and potent.

Succeedent houses 2,5,8, and 11—so-called because these houses follow on from the angular houses. They correspond to the fixed signs.

Cadent houses 3,6,9, and 12—cadent means "falling" and these houses correspond to the mutable signs. Planets situated in these houses are said to be at their least visible. However, this does not mean that planets in these houses are weak or inactive.

NATURAL HOUSE

If a planet is in its own, natural house then it is said to be strengthened. For example, a first-house Mars, a second-house Venus, or a third-house Mercury would all be planets in their natural houses.

FIRST HOUSE
Aries—Mars
The physical body, appearance, the ego and sense of self.

SECOND HOUSE
Taurus—Venus
Personal money matters and possessions, all material goods, food, practical resources.

THIRD HOUSE
Gemini—Mercury
Brothers and sisters, neighbors and neighborhood; local travel and all modes of local transport; communication—letters, the media, phones, computers, conversation, gossip, rumors; early education; traditionally known as the house of "the lower mind."

FOURTH HOUSE
Cancer—the Moon
Home, roots, origins, a parent—even though the Moon and Cancer are more

ACCIDENTAL DIGNITY

If a planet is in the house of the sign in which it is exalted, then this planet is said to be in accidental dignity. For example, a first-house Sun, as the Sun is exalted in Aries, or a tenth-house Mars, as Mars is exalted in Capricorn.

DERIVED HOUSES

This technique relates to locating concerns of other people in your chart. For example, your seventh house speaks of your partner and can represent your partner's first house. Your eighth house represents your partner's money and can represent your partner's second house. Your ninth house represents your partner's siblings and can represent your partner's third house, and so on. If I want to locate my sister's children I would take my third house (siblings) as my sister's first and then count to her fifth (children)—they are therefore located in my seventh house.

PLANETARY JOYS

The traditional planets each have a house in which they are said "to joy," i.e., rejoice, giving the planet concerned extra strength or positive values.

SUN	*Joys in the ninth*
MOON	*Joys in the third*
MERCURY	*Joys in the first*
VENUS	*Joys in the fifth*
MARS	*Joys in the sixth*
JUPITER	*Joys in the eleventh*
SATURN	*Joys in the twelfth*

associated with the mother, the fourth house is about our early years.

FIFTH HOUSE
Leo—the Sun
Children and all that we create; parties, hobbies, relaxation, holidays, and anything enjoyable; gambling and risk-taking; lovers, but key relationships belong to the seventh house.

SIXTH HOUSE
Virgo—Mercury
Day-to-day work and chores; crafts and skills; health matters; the house of service—anyone in our employment; those who serve their country, this is also the house of the armed forces; small animals.

SEVENTH HOUSE
Libra—Venus
Marriage and partnership, major, one-to-one relationships, either personal or business; open enemies; the house of the "significant other."

EIGHTH HOUSE
Scorpio—Mars and Pluto
Other people's money and resources, especially your partner's; death, legacies, and bequests; sex and the cycle of conception, birth, and decay; symbolic rebirth and transformation; the unconscious and all that is hidden or taboo; surgery.

NINTH HOUSE
Sagittarius—Jupiter
Traditionally known as the house of "the higher mind"; higher education, philosophy, search for meaning, astrology, religion, law; advertising and publishing; long-distance travel and means of transport, so especially planes; all things foreign.

TENTH HOUSE
Capricorn—Saturn
The other parent, who is often the breadwinner, as opposed to the homemaker; career, ambitions, and status; public life.

ELEVENTH HOUSE
Aquarius—Saturn and Uranus
The circle of people outside family and sexual relationships—friends, colleagues, and associates; social life, groups, societies, and organizations of all kinds; traditionally known as the house of "hopes and wishes"; ideals, social values, and political beliefs.

TWELFTH HOUSE
Pisces—Jupiter and Neptune
Traditionally known as the "vale of tears"—those who are lost to us, sacrifices, and seclusion; any place of confinement, such as hospitals or prisons; privacy or withdrawal; contemplation, mysticism, karma; hidden enemies, blind spots, self-undoing, and ambushes.

THE ANGLES

If you draw a line from the first house to the seventh, and from the fourth to the tenth, these axes mark out the important angles of the chart (see page 69). The subsequent trisection of the quadrants creates the inner house cusps and the 12 houses. The horoscopic wheel also acts as a 24-hour clock.

THE ASCENDANT *6 am (sunrise)*

Arguably the most important part of the horoscope, the Ascendant—or rising sign—is the sign rising over the eastern horizon at the time of birth. It therefore marks the beginning of the first house and is the doorway into any chart. This angle can be calculated only if the time of birth is known and the more accurate the birth time, the more accurate the horoscope.

All 12 signs of the zodiac rise over the eastern horizon in any 24-hour period. So, as a rough rule of thumb the Ascendant changes sign every two hours. However, owing to a phenomenon called Short Ascension or Long Ascension, some signs pass over the horizon more quickly than others. In the northern hemisphere the fastest rising signs are the first and the last—Aries and Pisces—with the signs either side gradually increasing speed. Libra and Virgo are the slowest rising signs. The overall picture is that in northern latitudes Gemini to Capricorn

inclusive are of Short Ascension and Cancer to Sagittarius are of Long Ascension. This pattern is inverted for southern latitudes. The timeline below gives you an approximate overall picture for the northern hemisphere.

WHAT DOES THE ASCENDANT SYMBOLIZE?

The Ascendant operates at several levels. Firstly, it symbolizes the face we present to the world, the characteristics we exhibit, and it is the first thing that others see or that we see about others. The Ascendant is about first impressions and is like the cover to a book. Only when we open the book do we find the "real" person inside. Although it is possible to guess someone's Sun sign, you have to dig under the surface first or you will guess only the rising sign. A Piscean with a Gemini Ascendant may appear chatty, sociable, witty, and resilient in public, modifying or concealing a nature that is much more

Aries and Pisces are the fastest-moving signs and Libra and Virgo are the

private, sensitive, reflective, or vulnerable. At another level our Ascendant acts as the lens through which we filter life. It symbolizes our approach to the world, how we find ourselves in relation to others, and how we operate. Someone with Virgo rising will put everything through an analytical sieve, inwardly questioning or testing the water as an initial response to a situation, a problem, or meeting someone.

As the angle to the first house, the physical body, the Ascendant has a big say in how we look. All the signs have their own physical characteristics and these can be replicated when the sign is rising. An Aries Ascendant may manifest as red hair or sharp features. Libra rising can bestow prettiness, softening the features. Physical appearance can be seen as a combination of the characteristics of the Ascendant, Sun, Moon, and planets in the first house.

THE DESCENDANT *6 pm (sunset)*
This marks the beginning of the seventh house and is opposite the Ascendant.

WHAT DOES THE DESCENDANT SYMBOLIZE?
If the Ascendant is "I" then the Descendant is "you"—your spouse, important sexual relationships, a business partner, or a significant other. It represents that which you seek from the other.

THE MIDHEAVEN *or M.C.(midday)*
M.C. stands for Medium Coeli, Latin for "the middle of the sky." This marks the beginning of the tenth house and moves at a rate of one degree every five minutes.

WHAT DOES THE MIDHEAVEN SYMBOLIZE?
In some horoscopes this angle is drawn as an arrow, pointing toward the heavens. The Midheaven symbolizes where you are going, your vocation, aspirations, and ambitions. It can speak of parental or social influence shaping your future.

THE I.C. (MIDNIGHT)
I.C. stands for Imum Coeli, which is Latin for "the bottom of the sky." This angle is always exactly opposite the M.C. and it marks the beginning of the fourth house.

WHAT DOES THE I.C. SYMBOLIZE?
The fourth house symbolizes both your origins and your final resting place. The I.C. speaks about your early upbringing and how you experienced parental influence at that time. This angle also represents your home and your base.

PLANETS ON ANGLES AND CUSPS
If a planet is conjunct an angle to within 5 degrees, it is said to be angular. Any planet conjunct an angle demands attention and often is the dominant feature of the chart.

If a planet is conjunct one of the inner house cusps to within 2 degrees, then it also invites attention, but to a lesser degree than the angles. Also, if a planet is 2 degrees or less away from the cusp of the next house, it belongs to that house. For example, if the fifth house cusp is 10 Aries and the Sun is at 8 Aries then this is a fifth-house Sun, not a fourth.

HOUSE RULERSHIP

When you look at a horoscope one of the first things you will notice is that certain houses are devoid of planets, but this does not mean that these houses are dormant or inactive.

An empty first house, for example, does not mean that there is no sense of self, just as an empty seventh house does not mean an absence of relationships. It simply means that we have to access the information about these houses in another way. Matters pertaining to the house in question are certainly described by any planets in that house but, more importantly, they are primarily described by the planet that rules the house.

LOCATING THE HOUSE RULERS

The ruler of the house is always the planet that rules the sign on the cusp of the house. The most important of these is the planet that rules the sign on the Ascendant, which is then taken as the chart ruler. So, if Virgo is rising, the individual will be ruled by Mercury,

This planetary conjunction at dawn shows the Moon on the right, Venus on the left, and Jupiter in the middle.

because Virgo is ruled by Mercury. If Leo is rising he or she will be ruled by the Sun, because Leo is ruled by the Sun, and so on. Planets in the first house can then be added to flesh out the picture but identifying and assessing the condition of the chart ruler is nearly always the first vital step in interpretation.

The same rules apply to each house. If the Descendant, for example, is Aries then the seventh house will be ruled by Mars, because Mars rules Aries, and the nature of relationships will be described by his condition. If the Ascendant is Gemini the Descendant will be Sagittarius, so relationships will be described by the condition of Jupiter, because Jupiter rules Sagittarius, and so on.

When considering a sign that has a co-ruler, always take the traditional planet as the primary significator and the co-ruler as the secondary. For instance, if Pisces sits on the seventh cusp then the nature of relationships will be described firstly by the condition of Jupiter, the traditional ruler of Pisces, and secondly by Neptune, the planet that co-rules Pisces.

Understanding the workings of house rulership is crucial to chart interpretation. If you use this system you can find everything in the horoscope and make sense of it. However, without attempting interpretation at this stage, here is Grace Kelly's horoscope as an example just for locating the house rulers (see opposite).

Locating the ruler of the Ascendant is the key that unlocks the door into the chart, and finding the subsequent house rulers enables you to find our way around the horoscope. At this stage you can start to ask the important question—"Who is this planet?" The more you venture into the machinery of the horoscope, the more you realize that it is not just about your personality or psychological make-up, but is also about your world and the people, events, and concerns that play roles in shaping your life.

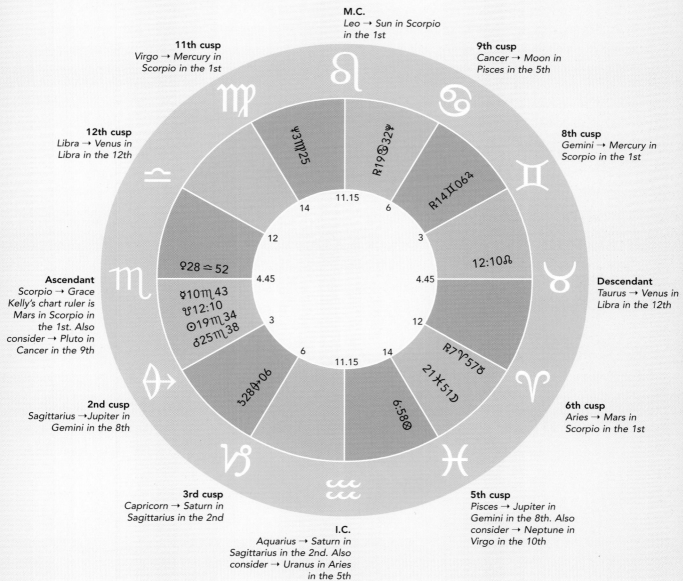

M.C.
Leo → Sun in Scorpio in the 1st

11th cusp
Virgo → Mercury in Scorpio in the 1st

9th cusp
Cancer → Moon in Pisces in the 5th

12th cusp
Libra → Venus in Libra in the 12th

8th cusp
Gemini → Mercury in Scorpio in the 1st

Ascendant
Scorpio → Grace Kelly's chart ruler is Mars in Scorpio in the 1st. Also consider → Pluto in Cancer in the 9th

Descendant
Taurus → Venus in Libra in the 12th

2nd cusp
Sagittarius →Jupiter in Gemini in the 8th

6th cusp
Aries → Mars in Scorpio in the 1st

3rd cusp
Capricorn → Saturn in Sagittarius in the 2nd

I.C.
Aquarius → Saturn in Sagittarius in the 2nd. Also consider → Uranus in Aries in the 5th

5th cusp
Pisces → Jupiter in Gemini in the 8th. Also consider → Neptune in Virgo in the 10th

ASPECTS

The aspects tell us about the relationships between the planets—whether or not they are connected, for good or ill, as allies or enemies.

As with planets in dignity or detriment, the astrologer needs to guard against judging positive aspects as "all good" and negative aspects as "all bad." Quite often it is the difficult aspects that symbolize our biggest challenges or obstacles, but these can also be the source of our personal growth and greatest achievements.

THE MAJOR ASPECTS

There are five major aspects (see below and right). The "orb" is the maximum distance allowed between the two for the aspect to be allowed. For example, the Sun at 12♌ and Mars at 16♌ would be a conjunction as the planets are 4 degrees apart. If we move Mars to 4♌ or 20♌—8 degrees either side of the Sun—this would still be a conjunction but at the maximum orb allowed. Beyond 4 or 20 degrees the planets are not conjunct, only in the same sign. The main point is that the tighter the orb, the more powerful the aspect.

Conjunction—planets next to each other, 8-degree orb. Harmonious or inharmonious depending on which planets are involved.

Opposition—planets 180 degrees apart, 8-degree orb. Inharmonious. A challenge to be faced, conflict.

Trine—planets 120 degrees apart, 8-degree orb. Planets are in the same element—positive, harmonious.

Square—planets 90 degrees apart, 8-degree orb. Planets in the same mode—inharmonious, a source of friction.

Sextile—planets 60 degrees apart, 6-degree orb. Planets in either feminine or masculine signs—harmonious.

THE MINOR ASPECTS

There are many minor aspects, but they are rarely used. The following are the most common ones. Your accuracy as an astrologer is not hindered if you do not utilize all the minor aspects.

Quinqunx—the Inconjunct—planets 150 degrees apart, 2-degree orb. This aspect is 30 degrees short of an opposition and speaks of blind spots, discord, and incompatibility. Inharmonious.

Semi-sextile—planets 30 degrees apart, 2-degree orb—half a sextile, planets in consecutive signs. Variable, depending on the planets involved.

Semi-square—planets 45 degrees apart, 2-degree orb. Inharmonious.

Sesquiquadrate—planets 135 degrees apart, 2-degree orb. Inharmonious.

FINDING THE ASPECTS

Aspect boxes are a popular but laborious way of locating the aspects in a chart. These grids list all of the planets across the

top and down the side, and then each planet is checked off against all of the other planets.

In chapter one I stressed the importance of learning the polarities, elements, and modes. This is because if you have this knowledge at your fingertips, you can spot aspects "at a glance."

Conjunctions: These are easy to spot as the two planets sit next to each other.

Trines: As long as the planets are within the orbs, those in the same element are always four signs apart—or 120 degrees —and therefore trine to each other. For example, the Sun at 12♌ and Mars at 12♈ would be trine to each other as both are in fire signs—the same element. In this case it is an exact trine as

they are also at the same degree. Mars anywhere between 4♈ and 20♈ would still make a trine as it would be within the allowable 8-degree orb, either side of the Sun at 12♌.

Squares and oppositions: Those in the same mode are either six signs apart—oppositions, or three signs apart (90 degrees)—squares. For example, the Sun at 12♌ and Mars at 12♉ would be in square to each other, as both are in fixed signs—the same mode. In this case it is an exact square, as they are also at the same degree. Mars anywhere between 4♉ and 20♉ still makes a square, as it is within the allowable 8-degree orb, either side of the Sun at 12♌. The Sun at 12♌ and Mars between 2 and 20♒ is an opposition.

Sextiles: These are always two signs apart (60 degrees), so they are either in feminine or masculine signs. For example, the Sun at 12♌ and Mars at 12♊, or the Sun at 12♌ and Mars at 12♎.

Quinqunxes: These are always five signs apart, (150 degrees). For example, the Sun at 12♌ and Mars at 12♑ or 12♓.

Semi-sextiles: These are always one sign apart (30 degrees). For example, the Sun at 12♌ and Mars at 12♋ or 12♍.

Semi-squares: These are always one and a half signs apart (45 degrees). For example, the Sun at 12♌ and Mars at 27♍.

Sesquiquadrates: These are always four and a half signs apart (135 degrees). For example, the Sun at 12♌ and Mars at 27♐.

DISSOCIATE ASPECTS

These are difficult to spot as dissociate aspects are those that are within orb but in the "wrong" signs. For example, the Sun at 12♌ and Mars at 16♌ is an obvious conjunction—four degrees apart and in the same sign. But if we move both of these planets forward by 15 degrees then we have the Sun at 27♌—still in the same sign—but Mars at 1♍. The planets are still four degrees apart but they now sit "across" two signs, making a dissociate conjunction.

The knack of spotting these "blind" aspects lies in picking up on planets that are either toward the end or the beginning of a sign—at late or early degrees. If you mentally move the planet backward or forward a few degrees, you will then see the dissociate aspects. For example:

- The Sun at 27♌ and Mars at 2♏—these are both fixed signs, four signs apart, which suggests a square, but this aspect is not 90 degrees apart.
- Move the Sun forward 5 degrees so that it becomes 2♍—we then see that it is in fact only two signs away, within a 6-degree orb—so it is a sextile.
- Move Mars back 5 degrees so that it becomes 27♎. We then see the planet as only two signs away, again making a sextile.

PARTILE ASPECTS

These are the opposite to dissociate aspects, as "partile" means exact to the degree and minute. Mars at 5♑40 and Venus at 5♑40 is a partile conjunction. Mercury at 2♊35 and Jupiter at 2♈35 is also a partile sextile. Partile aspects are rare but powerful, for good or ill, depending on the planets and aspects involved.

MUTUAL RECEPTION

Planets are in mutual reception if they are in each other's sign of dignity. For example, the Sun in Aries and Mars in Leo—the Sun is in Mars' sign and Mars is in the Sun's sign. This is a helpful relationship.

Mutual receptions are especially helpful when the planets concerned are in difficult signs. For example, the Moon in Scorpio and Mars in Cancer shows both planets in their sign of fall. However, they are also in each other's signs and the mutual reception indicates the possibility of alliance rather than enmity.

MIXED RECEPTION

Planets are in mixed reception when one is in the other's sign of dignity and the second is in the other's sign of exaltation. For example, the Moon in Leo and the Sun in Taurus—the Moon in the Sun's sign and the Sun in the Moon's sign of exaltation; or Venus in Capricorn and Saturn in Pisces—Venus in Saturn's sign and Saturn in Venus' sign of exaltation.

DISPOSITORS

Planet A is the "dispositor" of Planet B if Planet A is in Planet B's own sign. This is like a "one-way" mutual reception. For example, Mars is the dispositor of any planet in Aries or Scorpio, regardless of the sign Mars occupies. Jupiter is the dispositor of any planet in Sagittarius or Pisces, regardless of the sign Jupiter occupies. The dispositing planet is more powerful in this relationship.

APPLYING AND SEPARATING ASPECTS

An aspect is more powerful when it is applying—when the aspect is still being formed. This is determined by which planet is the swifter moving body. For example, the Moon at 4♍ and Pluto at 10♍ is an applying conjunction—the Moon is the swifter moving body and is therefore applying, or moving toward Pluto. This is also called perfecting.

The Moon at 14♍ and Pluto at 10♍ is a separating conjunction, as the Moon is separating—moving away from—Pluto.

Whether an aspect is applying or separating tells us if that aspect is increasing or decreasing in power, but this does not affect the aspect much in terms of natal interpretation. A Moon-Pluto conjunction is always a Moon-Pluto conjunction, regardless which side of Pluto the Moon may sit. However, understanding this principle is vital when working with progressions—predictions—as we will see in chapter six.

ASPECT PATTERNS

Aspect patterns are formed when more than two planets are linked together. As these patterns can be a dominant factor they can often form the crux of a chart.

STELLIUM

Three planets conjuncting each other in the same sign are a triple conjunction, but four or more planets conjuncting each other in the same sign constitute a stellium. For example, ☉4♉, ☽7♉, ♂12♉, ♃18♉. This places a strong focus on one sign and one or more particular houses.

T-SQUARE

This is very common and is formed by an opposition, with both planets making a square to a third. The third planet is often the focal point and can act as some kind of release valve from the opposition. The T-square will be either cardinal, fixed, or mutable, unless there are dissociate aspects involved, as illustrated below. Note the planets and houses involved—i.e. the rulership of the planets in question as well as the houses in which they fall.

THE GRAND CROSS

Unless there are dissociate aspects, this aspect pattern will be either cardinal, fixed, or mutable. Note the planets and houses involved. This is a stressful aspect pattern, "a cross to bear."

THE GRAND TRINE

This aspect pattern is formed by three planets in a triangle, so look for the presence of all three signs of the same triplicity (element). Unless there are dissociate aspects involved the grand trine will be in either fire, earth, air, or water. (The diagram below shows three water signs.) This pattern is not as harmonious as you might imagine, as there may be too much emphasis on one element. Consider the condition of the planets and houses that are involved.

THE KITE

If you locate a grand trine then see if there is an opposition to any of the three planets involved. If the opposing planet makes sextiles to the other two planets in the grand trine, you have a kite formation. This aspect pattern is surprisingly common

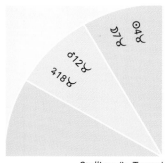

Stellium (in Taurus)

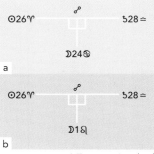

a) T-square (cardinal)
b) T-square (dissociate)

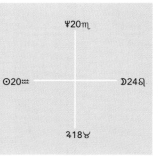

Grand cross (fixed)

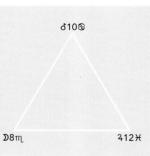

Grand trine (water)

and can hold considerable power and potential. Note the planets and houses involved and especially the condition of the planet making the opposition, the "handle" to the kite. (In the diagram below, the Sun is making the opposition.)

YOD, OR FINGER OF FATE

This is a less common aspect pattern as it involves two planets in quinqunx to a third planet. The first two planets are in sextile and the planet forming the point of the isosceles triangle is the focal point. As a quinqunx speaks of our blind spots this is a very difficult aspect pattern. It is the things that we don't see coming, such as accidents or illness. Consider the condition of the planets and houses involved.

STAR OF DAVID

This aspect pattern is extremely rare—I have never seen one in my own practice. Look for two grand trines, six planets all in sextile to each other, creating this harmonious, unifying pattern. Unless there are dissociate aspects involved, the Star of David will be in either masculine or feminine signs.

Each aspect pattern you locate will be different in terms of the signs, planets, and houses concerned, but the guidelines for assessment are the same.

- What is the condition of the focal planet(s)?
- Which planet is the strongest—by sign or house?
- Does the pattern include the chart ruler or ruler of the other angles?
- Does the pattern fall in angular houses or conjunct the angles?

Chapters one to three are designed to provide all the technical information that you need when starting to work with a horoscope. Understanding the symbolism of the planets in their signs and houses, the importance of house rulership, and identifying and assessing the strength of aspects and aspect patterns are the major components of natal chart interpretation—the preliminary work that is needed before you set the horoscope in motion with transits and progressions.

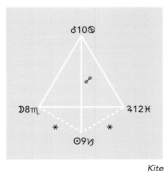

Kite

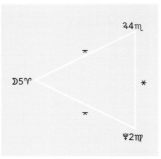

Yod or finger of fate

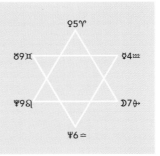

Star of David

The art of chart interpretation is twofold. As every horoscope is unique, the first step is to zoom in on what is important by identifying and prioritizing the different factors in play. Secondly, the art of interpretation demands that the astrologer convert this information into meaning. Through understanding the nature of symbolism, along with the skills of astrological craft, each horoscope tells its story when seen within the context of an individual's life and psyche.

SIGNIFICANCE & SYMBOLISM

LOCATING SIGNIFICANCE

"The beginner usually sees in a horoscope a mass of disconnected influences of every kind, and is entirely at a loss to know how to proceed. Usually he reads the description of planets in signs and houses and gets very little further, chiefly because of the lack of any method."

Vivian Robson, A Beginner's Guide to Practical Astrology

"Locating Significance" is a term coined by Maggie Hyde and Geoffrey Cornelius of the Company of Astrologers and it addresses the challenge of finding meaning when first considering a horoscope. The basic principle is that through the acquisition of craft, learning the nuts and bolts of horoscopes, the astrologer learns how to work creatively with each individual horoscope. It is an exercise that points the astrologer in the right direction, showing how to cut through the "mass of disconnected influences" so that the patterns and themes of each chart are revealed.

Locating significance is primarily an approach that teaches us how to prioritize, a way of zooming in on what is important rather than being sidetracked by minutiae. Its aim is to bring a chart to life, with the additional bonus that hours of painstaking analysis become a thing of the past.

The art of interpretation is every astrologer's goal and it is an elusive skill that we continuously strive to perfect. The above quotation from 1930 shows us that this problem is clearly not just a contemporary one. Every student of astrology reaches the point at which the learning process requires a creative leap—from the acquisition of facts and data to interpreting their meaning.

We can learn the vocabulary and grammar of another tongue but this doesn't automatically mean that we can speak that language. Vocabulary and grammar are the building blocks inherent in any language, just as planets, signs, houses, and aspects are the astrologer's building blocks, and the framework they provide is the bedrock of interpretation. To learn the basics of astrology—as explained in the first three chapters—is essentially to arm yourself with the tools of your trade. How to use those tools with skill is, as with any craft, a matter of time, application, and practice. But the sooner you can get the basics under your belt, so that they become fingertip knowledge, the sooner you will start to bridge the gap between information and meaning.

BRIDGING THE GAP

Every would-be astrologer, without exception, faces the frustration of learning how to calculate a chart, drawing it up, and then staring at it blankly in the hope that it will somehow offer up its treasure. I certainly remember this experience when I first started studying astrology and it seemed to me that everyone else in a class or lecture had a far better grasp and understanding than I did. In a kind of determined panic we review all the books supplying lists of keywords for planets in signs and houses, we fill in aspect boxes, religiously record the distribution of all the elements and modes, analyze every planet, and, when we still find ourselves struggling to make sense of it all, we then hear about all sorts of techniques which will yield the answers to all our problems.

This response is what astrologer Marc Edmund Jones refers to as "the regression of technique." Running after more and more ways of interpreting a chart is not the answer but simply a path going backward, taking us further away from the heart of a horoscope. It's no wonder that so many students give up on astrology when, in the face of a bewildering amount of conflicting information, they find that they are unable to "synthesize" the chart and conclude that interpretation is beyond them. In other words, they just can't see what it all means.

CHART SYNTHESIS

"Synthesis" is a word that is used a lot in astrology. It is often misleading, implying that there is some way of arriving at an understanding of the whole chart and that only when you understand the whole chart will you succeed in decoding its message. It suggests that every part of the horoscope—planets, angles, houses, nodes, and so on—has equal weight and that meshing them all together will then yield meaning. In pursuit of this supposedly infallible formula the astrologer more often than not falls into the trap of compiling endless lists of information. Any student who has already trodden this path will know that the result is all too often a mass of puzzling contradictions and inconsistencies.

Through the acquisition of craft, the astrologer can work creatively with each horoscope.

Preparation can easily get out of hand. There is little point in dissecting a horoscope by listing every detail and then making interpretations that can never be much more than a stab in the dark. Laborious notes are usually of little real value when actually face to face with a client. This is because only the client can provide the true context—his or her own story—so there is always a limit to how much the astrologer can know in advance with natal interpretation, that is, finding meaning in the birth chart. This also partly explains why preparing written charts is so difficult and essentially pointless. Astrology is not clairvoyance.

SIGNIFICANCE & SYMBOLISM

PREPARATORY CHECKLIST

Locating significance constitutes the work that the astrologer can do in advance. It is a guide, providing a flexible framework that allows the astrologer to establish the nature of the symbolism at work without leaping to interpretative conclusions. In fact, at this stage, it is vital that the astrologer does not make interpretations, as this preliminary preparation is still an objective exercise. Even though certain ideas and theories will start to take shape in your head, and these are worth noting, it is important not to lose sight of the fact that they are just ideas and theories, yet to be tested out.

When you are working with a new horoscope the preparatory work can be reduced to a ten-point checklist, the tenth of which relates to timing measures—the techniques for prediction. The example horoscopes in this chapter will deal with the first nine points.

This checklist may at first seem a lot of work but, once you have the basics as fingertip knowledge, this approach is incredibly quick. With practice you can run through these points in minutes, laying the groundwork that no computer package is capable of. Astrological software is helpful only in speeding up the mathematics of what you already know how to do, such as calculating the natal chart or listing aspects. It is of very little use when it comes to interpretation, as you will know if you have ever sent off for a computerized chart.

Once you have completed the exercise for locating significance, the technical preparation—with the exception of the timing measures—is complete. You will also have made a start on the interpretative work by assessing and prioritizing the main features of a chart, without the pressure of leaping from this stage to offering an interpretation of the whole chart. You have instead subjected the horoscope to the discriminating test of the astrologer's craft and identified what is most important.

Learning to use this guide will demonstrate to you how astrology works. It reminds you that the first task of the astrologer is not to know in advance but to establish symbolic relevance. For this reason it is a helpful exercise to start with the horoscopes of famous people, to see how their charts speak of what they are known for. Often you will find that you are able to locate the "signature" of the chart—a striking feature that sums up the nature of someone's achievements or reputation—or at least establish a theme.

The horoscopes that follow have been chosen to show how the exercise for locating significance works in practice, demonstrating how the features of the chart and the ideas or themes they suggest can be condensed to just a single page of notes.

LOCATING SIGNIFICANCE

Simplify the technical preparation with this ten-point checklist:

1 DRAWING UP THE CHART

I use astrological software to make my calculations but I always draw the chart up in my own hand—ten planets, nodes, Part of Fortune, but nothing else. To me there is nothing more disorienting and off-putting than looking at a chart crisscrossed with aspect lines or notes. Other information should be written on a separate sheet. I particularly dislike computer-drawn charts, although some are better presented than others, as I feel that they are somewhat clinical and impersonal, especially for the client. But far more importantly, the real reason for drawing up a chart in your own hand is that it is, in my opinion, an indispensable and deeply satisfying ritual. There is something dynamic about watching the chart take shape under your hand rather than looking at the finished article appearing out of the printer. By drawing the chart up in your own hand you are allowing the chart to come to life in a way that is gradual and informative.

2 LOOK FOR SIGNIFICANT FEATURES

Looking at the whole chart for the first time, note if anything immediately demands attention. If you have drawn the chart up yourself, your own hand may already have guided you to what is important. A stellium, or a planet on any of the angles or the inner house cusps, are obvious examples, but note anything that strikes you as significant.

3 LOCATE THE CHART RULER

This is the planet that rules the sign on the Ascendant. What is its condition? You will ask this question again and again in chart interpretation. A planet's condition is assessed by three key questions:
1 What sign is the planet in—is it friend, foe, or neither?
2 Which house is the planet in?
3 What positive or negative aspects does it receive from other planets? While the whole chart is unique to an individual, the chart ruler is the

"significator." When assessing the condition of other planets, note which house(s) the planet rules.

4 NOTE THE CONDITION OF THE SUN AND THE MOON.

Note the condition of the lights by sign, house, and aspect.

5 NOTE ANY ASPECT PATTERNS AND DRAW THEM PICTORIALLY

This was illustrated in the previous chapter. Locate the focal planet of the pattern and note its condition and the house(s) it rules.

6 NOTE ANY MAJOR OR MINOR ASPECTS AMONG THE REMAINING PLANETS

At this stage it is crucial to prioritize. Aspects involving the slow-moving outer planets can last for years and are therefore not particular to any one chart, such as a sextile between Neptune and Pluto. The outer planets assume importance only if they are on angles or involved with the personal planets, such as Pluto on the

Ascendant, a Sun-Neptune conjunction, a Moon square Uranus, and so on.

7 NOTE ANY UNASPECTED PLANETS

This is a planet that stands alone, unintegrated into the rest of the chart.

8 NOTE ANY PLANETS THAT ARE IN MUTUAL RECEPTION.

This is when two planets are in each other's signs.

9 NOTE THE PROMINENCE OF THE NODES, PART OF FORTUNE, OR ANY FIXED STARS

These may act as possible testimonies to patterns or themes.

10 LOCATE THE TRANSITS AND PROGRESSIONS FOR SPECIFIC EVENTS OR DATES

See the following two chapters.

EXAMPLE HOROSCOPES

Whether you are a beginner in astrology or an advanced student, it is always educational, and often fascinating, to study charts of celebrities. When it comes to preparing work for clients you can still lay the groundwork at a technical level, pointing yourself in the right direction, but with well-known people you have the advantage of already having some context in which to frame the astrology.

The following examples and anecdotes are not intended as comprehensive case histories. These exercises illustrate how to identify the astrological factors in play, which then allow the astrologer to make "takes"—that is, to put forward possible interpretations of the symbolism. I have also expanded upon some points of astrological symbolism that may be helpful for future reference and for other charts.

CATHERINE ZETA-JONES

Actress, famous in her own right and for being married to actor Michael Douglas. See page 61 for her chart.

THE NINTH HOUSE

With five planets in the ninth we are immediately drawn into this sector of the chart. Here we find Pluto conjunct the ninth cusp and a stellium in Libra—the Sun, Uranus, Mercury, and Jupiter. The importance of the stellium is underlined by the fact that, with Sagittarius rising, it includes Jupiter, the chart ruler. Jupiter in the ninth is also strong by being in its natural house. This grouping alerts the astrologer to the importance of ninth-house issues, which warrant investigation.

CHART RULER

Jupiter is conjunct most closely to Mercury, in this case ruler of the seventh. (Rulers of the first and seventh together indicate closeness of partner and importance of marriage.) Mercury and Jupiter are both in Libra, the sign of partnership, in the ninth house of all things foreign (married to a foreigner and resident in his country).

SUN CONJUNCT URANUS

This is the second major feature of the stellium in the ninth. The Sun is weak by sign—in its sign of fall—but strong by house—it joys in the ninth. (The ninth house points abroad, but also to legal concerns. Zeta-Jones was involved in a controversial (Uranus) lawsuit (Jupiter/ninth house) over the publication of her wedding photos.)

ASPECT PATTERN 1
A Dissociate T-Square

The Moon is in Pisces opposite Pluto in Virgo, both in dissociate square to Mars in early degrees of Capricorn. The Sun conjunct Uranus is pulled into the pattern:

◆ The Sun is in dissociate conjunction with Pluto
◆ The Sun conjunct Uranus, both in dissociate opposition to the Moon
◆ The Sun and Uranus both square Mars
◆ Mercury on the edge of the pattern, conjunct Uranus and square Mars

This is a complex pattern that is difficult to interpret without the individual's own words and story, that is, the true context for the symbolism. At a speculative level, a T-square speaks of some kind of inner or outer conflict that needs to be addressed and resolved. In this example, the dissociate aspects to a first house, exalted Mars would suggest the battle for personal advancement that has not been fought without a cost.

MOON/PLUTO OPPOSITION IN T-SQUARE MEDIATED BY NEPTUNE IN SCORPIO

Here we see the Neptune-Pluto sextile that is generational, but in this case it is part of a powerful pattern with the Moon in Pisces. Neptune mediates the Moon-Pluto opposition, which means that this planet aspects both of the other planets. In this case, Neptune is sextile Pluto and trine the Moon. (Pisces/Neptune factors often feature in the charts of actors. In this case Neptune may symbolize the creative outlet for an intense, sensitive, emotional nature. Moon/Pluto contacts also often point to an intense or even obsessive mother/child relationship but psychological "takes" can be explored only in consultation.)

ASPECT PATTERN 2
A Grand Trine in Earth

Mars is exalted in Capricorn, intercepted in the first, trine Venus in Virgo (Venus' sign of fall), and Saturn in Taurus. The Mars trine Venus is the tightest aspect of the chart being just 17 minutes of arc apart. (Mars and Venus are universal for relationships, so this aspect testifies to a strong marriage theme.) Mars is the most

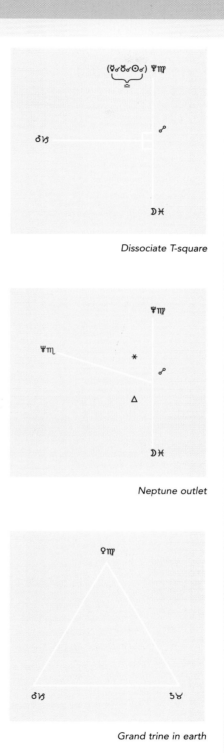

Dissociate T-square

Neptune outlet

Grand trine in earth

important part of the Grand Trine, being exalted and angular. (She was described by the director of the movie *Chicago*, in which she starred, as "the incredibly hard-working Catherine Zeta-Jones," a perfect showing of Mars in Capricorn.) Saturn in Taurus in the fourth speaks of her family roots and sense of Welsh heritage.

MUTUAL RECEPTION

There is a mutual reception between Mercury in Libra in the ninth and Venus in Virgo in the eighth—helpful, as Venus is in fall and also in a dissociate square to Neptune. (Mercury is the ruler of the seventh, so advancement through the partner is important. This feature also suggests keeping a dying (eighth house) language (Mercury) alive—she is fluent in Welsh.)

NO PLANETS IN FIRE

Often a missing element can symbolize that which we need to seek outside of ourselves—in our work, interests, or through our relationships, as discussed later in this chapter. An absence of fire may, for example, indicate a nature that seeks drama, passion, or excitement.

SYLVIA PLATH

Writer and poet. Married to poet Ted Hughes, with whom she had two children. They were separated at the time of her suicide at the age of 30.

THE SEVENTH HOUSE

With four planets in the seventh house we are immediately drawn into this sector of the chart. Here we find the Moon in Libra and a triple conjunction of Neptune, Jupiter, and Venus, intercepted in the seventh in Virgo. Neptune and Jupiter are in detriment, Venus is in fall. Jupiter is almost exactly conjunct the unlucky South Node.

Here is a troubled seventh house (marriage) with both benefics and Neptune unhappily placed. The quest for perfection, unrealistic dreams, and expectations would lead continually to disappointment, feeding the depression that would eventually result in her suicide.

AQUARIUS ASCENDANT

With such a late degree rising, at the very end of Aquarius, it is always worth questioning the accuracy of the birth

Sylvia Plath's troubled seventh house reflects her disappointments and depression, which led to suicide.

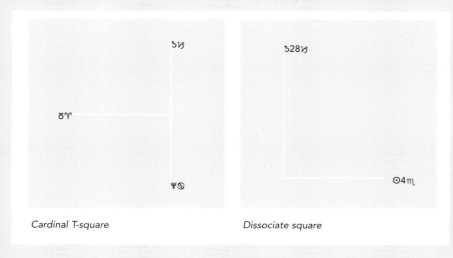

Cardinal T-square   Dissociate square

time (see "A Tale of Rectification" later in this chapter). With Sylvia Plath the Aquarius Ascendant seems to work—she struggled with the classic Aquarius/Uranus split between brilliance and instability and she was known for her systematic approach to writing, constantly using a thesaurus. More importantly this Ascendant gives Saturn as the chart ruler—strong by sign, in dignity in Capricorn, and strong by house, as Saturn joys in the 12th, but afflicted by aspect:

- Saturn as part of a cardinal T-square—Saturn opposing Pluto, both squaring Uranus, the co-ruler of the chart
- Saturn also in a dissociate square to the Sun in Scorpio in the eighth. (This configuration is a fitting symbol for her best-known work, *The Bell Jar*, which is about the sense of isolation and disconnection that results from severe depression and is based on her own experiences.) The T-square can also be seen to describe the drastic electric shock treatment that she was subjected to—chart ruler in the house of confinement opposite Pluto, both square Uranus (shocks/electricity) in Aries (the head).

MERCURY IN SCORPIO, CONJUNCT NINTH-HOUSE CUSP

This planet holds a pivotal position in the chart by holding aspects with no less than five of the other planets—square Mars, trine Pluto, sextile Venus and Jupiter, and quinqunx Uranus. We can see Mercury (writing) in Scorpio (powerful words, morbid fascination with death/rebirth), conjunct the ninth cusp (academic brilliance). The mixed bag of aspects can also be seen as her compulsion to write and her ambition to succeed. Also, Mercury, ruler of the fourth house, shows how her early life was blighted by the death of her father, which became a major source of her troubles.

SUN IN SCORPIO IN MUTUAL RECEPTION WITH MARS IN LEO

One way to explore a mutual reception is to swap the planets by sign but hold the degree, and then see if anything interesting happens. In this example, the Sun moves to 4 Leo and Mars moves to 21 Scorpio, therefore conjuncting the powerfully placed Mercury. This suggests a "move" she could make to express (Mercury) her anger/passion (Mars). It seems that she did this in her writing, venting her spleen to the extent that Ted Hughes sealed much of her personal writing until after the death of her mother.

MOON UNASPECTED IN LIBRA IN THE SEVENTH

The Moon (emotional needs) is in the sign of partnership and in the house of partnership, but unintegrated into the rest of her chart. (A testimony to her loneliness and the failure of her marriage.)

BILL GATES

Chairman and Chief Software Architect of Microsoft.

CHART RULER

With Cancer rising, Bill Gates' chart ruler is the Moon in single-minded, go-getting Aries, conjunct the Mid-heaven (status, purpose, and ambition). The Moon is trine Uranus (originality, innovation, and technology) in the first house (personal charisma). Uranus is only 17 minutes of arc short of a dissociate conjunction with the Ascendant. Even if this conjunction is not allowed by the strict rules of astrological craft, it can still be established that Uranus is "rising" in the first, and is therefore powerfully placed. The Moon-Uranus fire trine close to the angles can be seen as the signature of the chart.

THE MOON OPPOSITE MARS IN LIBRA

Mars is in one of its signs of detriment—but with the Moon in Mars' sign of Aries, Mars disposits the powerfully placed angular Moon, and is also ruler of the Aries Midheaven. Mars also disposits the Sun in Scorpio—so it is the dispositor of both of the lights. (This shows personal drive and determination, the cut and thrust of business, the power to succeed.) Mars in turn is conjunct Mercury in Libra, showing an expert negotiator. This feature also reflects the title of his book, *Business @ the Speed of Thought*—speed (Mars), thought (Mercury), and the ability to conduct business and liaise (Libra).

JUPITER CONJUNCT PLUTO IN LEO IN THE SECOND

Jupiter expands whatever it touches, in this case Pluto, both in lavish Leo in the second house (here we see Pluto's connection to wealth, as explained in chapter two). Bill Gates was a billionaire by the age of 31. He is also a philanthropist and has donated millions to various causes, echoing Jupiter's symbolism of generosity and doing everything on a large scale. Jupiter, with a 12-year cycle, catches up with slow-moving Pluto every 13 years. Bill Gates is born just as the Jupiter-Pluto conjunction is applying, or perfecting, as it is exact just five days after his birthday. Note also that Pluto is closely conjunct the benefic and fortunate fixed star of Regulus at 29 Leo that stands for ambition, honor, success, and leadership.

SUN/PLUTO MUTUAL RECEPTION

The potency of the Jupiter-Pluto conjunction is underlined by the mutual reception between the Sun in Scorpio, ruler of the second, and Pluto in Leo. Following the same method as demonstrated for Sylvia Plath, we can swap the planets but hold the degree. So Pluto "moves" to 28 Scorpio and the Sun "moves" to 5 Leo. In this horoscope the Sun is square the dominant Uranus in the first, but the mutual reception demonstrates a move that puts the Sun conjunct Uranus. This shows wealth and success through innovative technology.

VENUS CONJUNCT SATURN IN SCORPIO IN THE FIFTH

This is the second striking conjunction in Bill Gates' horoscope, with the two planets just over 1 degree apart. Venus is in detriment—but helped by a mutual reception with Mars in Libra—and conjunct Saturn, ruler of the seventh, so this feature relates directly to marriage and partnership. (Venus-Saturn contacts—or Moon-Saturn—can delay marriage, especially in a man's chart. Bill Gates married Melinda French Gates on 1 January 1994, at the age of 39. Saturn as ruler of the seventh sometimes signifies an older partner, or a partner who is Saturnian in other ways.)

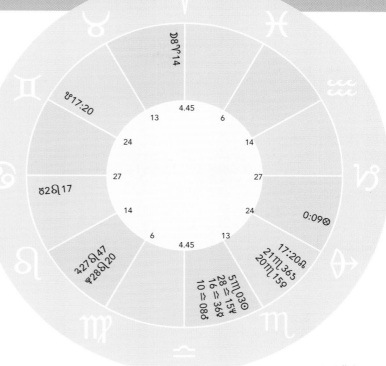

In Bill Gates' chart, the Sun conjunct Uranus shows wealth and success through innovative technology.

PRACTICE MAKES PERFECT

As with all astrological study, the art of locating significance is an acquired skill. The astrologer identifies key factors not through an instinctive act but by repeatedly applying the tools of the trade. In the early stages of learning you will probably gain more from this exercise than any other. Firstly, by practicing this approach you reinforce your working knowledge of the components of a chart—planets, signs, aspects, and houses. Secondly, locating significance reminds the astrologer to use the horoscope as a constant frame of reference.

For example, with Catherine Zeta-Jones' chart, the astrologer can ask, "Where do I see the foreign partner, where do I see strong family roots?" With Sylvia Plath you can ask, "Where do I see her depression and psychiatric treatment, where do I see her literary brilliance?" With Bill Gates, "Where do I see the technological wizard, where do I see the millionaire?" In other words, the chart is the person

and the person is the chart. If you apply this exercise to your own horoscope, and to those of friends and family, you will learn a great deal.

When it comes to preparing charts for clients, you will not have this same context but, again, the person is the chart and he or she will speak the chart to you. The astrologer's first task is to listen and to locate the person's story in the chart. Preparing the exercise for locating significance beforehand enables the astrologer to convert universal symbolism into the particular at the time of a consultation, thereby breathing life into the chart in a way that is both technically accurate and meaningful.

THE NATURE OF SYMBOLISM

Locating significance is a vital part of the astrologer's craft for two reasons. Firstly, it teaches the astrologer to be sure-footed at a technical level and, secondly, this preparatory work provides the framework for establishing relevant symbolism. These are the two sides of the astrological coin.

As the famous 17th century astrologer William Lilly says in *Christian Astrology*, "the exact way of judicature in astrology is, first, by being perfect in the nature of the planets and the signs," but from thereon what counts is your ability to step beyond the parameters of "keywords," and use symbolism creatively in interpretation.

WHAT IS SYMBOLISM?

In the early stages of study there is a tendency to assign predetermined meanings to combinations of planets in signs—keywords—only to find that this does not work beyond a certain point. This is because a symbol can never stand for just one thing. If it did, it would become simply a name or a sign for something that is already known. A symbol is rich with possibilities and always open to interpretation. Symbolism essentially represents that which is unknown.

This apparent paradox lies at the heart of astrology. How can we learn astrology if it is unknowable? What can be more frustrating for the student who thinks he or she has discovered the meaning of Jupiter in Gemini in the ninth house, only to find that this combination means something different in another horoscope? We quickly learn that the more we try to make a symbol mean one thing, the more it refuses to play. Symbolism cannot be neatly boxed, and attempts to categorize render it flat and lifeless. Yet to say that a symbol could mean many kinds of things is different from saying that anything goes.

UNIVERSAL VERSUS PARTICULAR

When understanding astrological symbolism—or any symbolism—the key issue lies in seeing the essential difference between the universal and the particular. In a nutshell, universal symbolism is objective and speaks of that which is already known—such as Jupiter ruling the law—whereas particular symbolism is subjective and dependent on context, that is, a symbol showing a certain event or person in an individual's life.

Our most important frame of reference is always the bigger picture. Although Jupiter in Gemini in the ninth house can mean many things this combination will nevertheless always speak of that which is "Jupiterian" and that which is "Geminian" within a ninth-house context. And just because Jupiter is in detriment in Gemini doesn't automatically make this bad news. In the early stages of study this "not knowing" may be frustrating but eventually it becomes the most magical part of working with charts. Read the following two chart anecdotes with the knowledge that Jupiter rules the higher mind and all things foreign; Gemini rules communication and speaks of duality or multiplicity; and the ninth house rules travel, education, and religion.

In the first chart, Jupiter in Gemini in the ninth was well-aspected—in a positive relationship with several other planets. This chart was of a woman working abroad in an embassy who spoke three languages, had two degrees, and was highly successful.

In the second chart, Jupiter in Gemini in the ninth house was the focal point of a troublesome T-square. This was the chart of a young woman who had been expelled from four colleges, at home and abroad, for rebellious behavior. She was bilingual. She had also rejected the religion she was born into and wanted to emigrate.

When getting to grips with how symbolism works it is helpful to remember that the planets are not causal. In themselves they do not make you be any particular way or do any particular thing.

> *"Signs are small measurable things, but interpretations are illimitable."*
>
> George Eliot, Middlemarch

Astrology assigns meaning through the act of rendering the planets symbolic, so think of a horoscope as a mirror, reflecting back to you what is already happening. Neither can we lose sight of the fact that symbolism is essentially fluid, lively, dynamic, and not without a sense of humor. The following story illustrates this point and also shows why trying to categorize personalities by Sun signs alone amounts to psychological typecasting and doesn't work.

LEO OR VIRGO?

A client whose Sun sign was Leo wanted to know why he was so "un-Leo-like," so I explained that his Ascendant was in Virgo, the sign after Leo. Consecutive signs often work as opposites, so whereas Leo is known for being the center of attention, big-hearted, and bossy, Virgo is known for being exacting and analytical. I explained that with Virgo rising, his ruling planet was

Mercury, and this planet was also in Virgo and in the 12th house, the house of confinement, along with his Leo Sun.

The 12th house is traditionally the realm of loss, tears, sacrifice, or self-undoing. The Sun cannot really shine in the 12th house, and with the overlay of Virgo, I wasn't surprised that he didn't identify with his leonine side. As I drew out these details he became increasingly amused. Why? He explained that he worked in a hospital, a 12th-house institution, in a restricted area. He worked with mercury every day, fixing and maintaining blood pressure machines—a highly skilled and exacting profession—and as mercury is poisonous the laboratory was open only to a small number of staff. The symbolism of a planet in

a sign in a house, in this case his ruling planet Mercury in Virgo in the 12th house, fitted like a glove.

A good rule to follow when locating symbolism is to go for the obvious. If you are dealing with the law, religion, or travel, then seek Jupiter or the ninth

house. If you hear of frustration or disappointment, then check out Saturn. If someone tells you they quit their job in a moment of impulse, look for Uranus, and so on. The following stories are examples of how symbolism acted as the key to astrological judgment.

HOUSE HUNTING

Some years ago a friend was desperately looking for somewhere to live and she took me to see the apartment she had in mind. As there were other people interested, she wanted to know if astrology could tell her if she would live in this property or another. As it was such a specific question I resorted to horary astrology—a branch of astrology that involves casting a chart for the moment a question is asked. It is not within the scope of this book to cover the technicalities of horary astrology, but, in this example, all you need to know is its most striking feature.

In the chart I went straight for the ruler of the fourth house—the home—which was Venus in Leo. In horary astrology, one of the most important factors in judgment depends on the Moon, its separating (last) aspect, and its applying (next) aspect. In this chart the Moon was in Gemini, suggesting a choice of two homes. It was separating from a square to Saturn in Pisces and applying to a sextile of Venus in Leo.

Having seen the apartment, the answer was obvious. It was run down and needed to be painted and decorated. Even with the Venusian investment of care and money, of which she had little, I couldn't see that this place would ever be described by Venus in Leo. It was dark (Saturn) and damp

(Pisces), so clearly she was leaving this place behind her—the Moon separating from Saturn—and would find an apartment that would be described by Venus in Leo—the Moon's next aspect. Venus (beauty) in Leo (comfort, luxury, and, being the Sun's own sign, light) promised that she would find somewhere much better, which she did.

A TALE OF RECTIFICATION

Rectification is the art of deciding on a horoscope when the time of birth is unsure or unknown. It is a complex area of astrology, but it can be helpful when making minor adjustments that lead to major changes, which then assist our interpretations.

A new client rang to make an appointment and gave her time of birth as 2.00 am. When I drew up the chart I found that at 1.59 am the Ascendant clicked over from Gemini to Cancer. When we met I opened the consultation with a query about the accuracy of her birth time, as it was unlikely to be exactly 2.00 am, and did she know if she had been born just before or just after this time? She didn't know but immediately whipped out her cell phone—a very Gemini thing to do—and rang her mother, but there was no answer.

The Ascendant rules the physical body, so I studied her appearance. Her eyes were bright and animated and I also noticed that she spoke quickly, striking up a conversation without any trouble. Again, this pointed to Gemini, but she also had a third house Sun—the house that naturally correlates to Gemini and would give a flavor of this sign—so I probed a little further.

I tried another tack. If Cancer were rising this would put Capricorn on the Descendant, so her relationships would be ruled by her Saturn in Pisces. If Gemini were rising this would put Sagittarius on the Descendant, so her relationships would be ruled by her Jupiter in Gemini. I focused on Jupiter and asked if she had ever had any foreign boyfriends? Her immediate answer was, "Oh yes, lots." Jupiter

(foreigners) in Gemini (lots) made complete sense. Transits and progressions (predictive techniques) also confirmed that Jupiter was the ruler of her Descendant, so I was able to rectify the chart by a few minutes to give an Ascendant of 29 degrees Gemini instead of 0 degrees Cancer.

THE WRONG CHART WORKING

On the other end of the scale from rectifying a chart by a few crucial minutes is the risk of having a chart that is wrong to begin with. Every astrologer will have some experience of having worked unknowingly with the wrong data, either from the astrologer's error or from a client supplying the wrong time of birth. There is a heart-stopping moment when you realize that you have the wrong chart and, if you have already calculated it and given interpretations, wondered if you have got it completely wrong. Will you have to ditch your work, go back to the client shamefaced, and start again? The answer is—not necessarily. Why not?

You need to ask: what is the "right" chart to begin with? In *The Moment of Astrology* Geoffrey Cornelius points out the purely logistical and practical hurdles of securing reliable data: "With all the opportunities there are for error, compounded by the hazy memories of mothers, wrong records, time-zone teasers, calculation catastrophes and general sloppiness by the astrologer, getting an accurate horoscope based on reliable data sometimes appears to be a noteworthy achievement."

The astrologer assumes that the horoscope is "right" as long as there is no uncertainty about the data, yet the wrong chart can, and often does, work— not just at a superficial level but with transits and progressions as well. This does not mean that birth data is irrelevant but, under the umbrella of the symbolic world, we cannot assume that the only source of data is "clock" time. In astrological practice we must always be alive to the way in which charts "come up" for us. Just the act of engaging with astrology connects us with something beyond ourselves and there is also the "owning" of the symbols. In other words, when a piece of astrological symbolism comes alive for us personally, even if it does not result from the "right" chart, it then directly relates to us because we see our own situation being reflected back to us. That which has chosen to show itself—like the turn of a Tarot card—becomes important and becomes the story. The following is an example from my own experience that showed this phenomenon very clearly.

A friend lived in Egypt for several years and had an Egyptian boyfriend. The relationship was mostly very happy and marriage was on the cards. When I cast his horoscope I was delighted to find that his Moon was in Sagittarius—the foreign woman—and, even better, that it was conjunct her Sagittarius Ascendant. When one person's Sun or Moon is conjunct the other person's Ascendant or Descendant this is considered to be textbook synastry, or compatibility.

However, the following year I discovered that, owing to haphazard methods of recording a birth, I had been given the wrong time and date. Not only was his Moon not conjunct her Ascendant, it wasn't even in Sagittarius. His Moon was in Capricorn, the same sign as her Saturn. And as the relationship ended up failing because needs on either side could not be fulfilled, I suspect that his Moon was probably very close to her Saturn (denial) by degree as well.

The important point is that the discovery of having the wrong chart was symbolic in itself as it coincided with the beginning of the breakdown of the relationship, a factor in which was his decision that he needed a more conventional (Capricorn) woman (Moon). But the "wrong" chart was "right" for a long time, that is, it gave an accurate image of the nature of the relationship, an image that cracked only when the "rightness" of the relationship itself was called into question. There is no causal principle at work here. The Moon in Sagittarius being supplanted by the Moon in Capricorn, the disappearance of the textbook synastry, did not make the relationship go wrong. The revelation of the wrong data and the rot setting in were synonymous, the symbolism accurately reflecting their experience and reality.

MISSING ELEMENTS

An element is considered to be absent if it is not found in the personal planets—the Sun through to Saturn. This means that none of the personal planets is in a water, fire, air, or earth sign. Exploring the symbolism of a missing element has often proved to be profitable. Even someone totally new to astrology can often connect quickly and easily with the concepts of fire, earth, air, and water. It is also a good example of how the same symbolism can manifest in different ways and remain appropriate and relevant.

However, we need to tread carefully when talking about a missing element. For instance, the element of water symbolizes our emotions and feelings, so what does it mean if someone has no water? It would be silly to suggest that someone has no feelings. On the contrary, the astrologer would need to investigate how the emotional side of life may have been neglected or repressed, why someone might feel that he or she has no "right" to feelings, why a person might struggle with empathy, and so on. As with any attempt at interpretation, the astrologer needs to open up the discussion so that it is investigative and therapeutic, never critical, always asking, "What is this telling me?"

A missing element often symbolizes that which you need to seek outside of yourself, such as through your work or relationships. It is surprising how often a missing element is to be found on the Descendant, underlining the theme of finding a quality through "the other." Very often we unconsciously find a way of compensating for what the missing element symbolizes. A friend with no water in her chart is an excellent psychotherapist, claiming the world of feelings through her work. Another friend has no earth in her chart but has learned how to make, build, and grow things. If someone doesn't find a way of compensating, astrology can show the person how.

WHERE'S THE FIRE?

The element of fire is associated with warmth, enthusiasm, intuition, and the ability to inspire and make things happen. If fire is missing in the personal planets, then the individual may still be a perfectly friendly or lively person, but may feel the lack of fiery qualities in some area of his or her life.

One client without any fire told me that his wife's main criticism of him was that he never really seemed "to let go." Although he loved her it was difficult for him to demonstrate this to her with real passion. The feelings were there but his fear of "losing control" was stronger. Neither could he deal with other heated emotions, especially anger. His Mars (passion and anger) in detriment in Taurus (fixed earth) bore witness to this block. Or, more accurately, the absence of fire acted as a testimony to issues flagged up by a troubled Mars. When I asked him how he handled his anger he replied, "Other people explode. I implode. It all goes inside," and, more importantly, "I allow others to get angry on my behalf." The latter statement is a typical expression of a missing element, revealing how the qualities of that element are found outside of the person, embodied in others. In this case, the man found others to act out his anger and passion for him.

With a woman in her late forties the absence of fire translated into literally no warmth—she had always suffered with the cold and poor circulation. She also found it difficult to "circulate" and had never made friends easily. She was very cautious and frugal, found little in life to get excited about, did not act spontaneously or feel passionate about things, and had suffered from depression. Although the absence of *joie de vivre* could be located in other factors in her chart, it was the idea of missing fire that made the most sense to her, and of how she could compensate for it that was the most helpful.

A more cheerful picture of missing fire was shown in a friend's chart. It made total sense to him, especially in terms of how he had compensated for the missing element. It turned out that he had always been attracted by fire, his home was overflowing with candles, he loved real fires, and he was fascinated with lighting of all kinds.

At an emotional level the idea of missing fire as the stifling of impulses clarified his understanding of his early experiences of undemonstrative parents and of having too much responsibility as a child. For him the missing element was found on the Descendant. With Gemini rising, he has Sagittarius on the Descendant (which marks the seventh house, representing relationships), so his partner is described by the ruling planet of Sagittarius: Jupiter, and she is, in fact, a volatile, confident, energetic, headstrong, and larger-than-life character.

The horoscope captures the moment of birth and is therefore also known as the nativity. When looking to the future, the astrologer must first understand the nature of transits—how the planets move on after the moment of birth, how their positions on any given date compare to the natal chart, and how this activity manifests in real life. This chapter also looks at the importance of lunations—new and full Moons—and eclipses, and how this symbolism assists our understanding of the horoscope.

TRANSITS & PREDICTION

WORKING WITH TRANSITS

"One perceives a subterranean current, one feels the grip of destiny, striking coincidences occur and the world is full of signs: such things...can indeed be the shadows of a real and not yet apprehended metamorphosis. Coming events do cast shadows."

Iris Murdoch, The Black Prince

The previous four chapters have dealt with the horoscope as a symbolic picture of the heavens viewed on the date and time of birth and from the place of birth. At this stage the astrologer assesses the strengths and weaknesses of the chart by locating significance at a technical level, as covered in chapter four, and also takes the first steps in identifying what is called natal promise. In other words, the astrologer starts to interpret the chart by speaking of likely personality traits, the nature of the individual's relationships, work, health issues, financial matters, and so on, treating the horoscope as a frozen moment in time.

Whenever I am with a new client I always start by explaining that the horoscope works on two levels. Firstly, the birth chart is often referred to as "the nativity," and the person as "the native." The nativity captures the position of the planets and angles at the moment of birth but, once that moment has passed, every-thing continues to move on. The second level of interpretation treats the horoscope as a mechanism in perpetual motion that symbolizes the unfolding and development of the native's life.

If the nativity is the picture, transits and progressions are the movie. Looking at how the chart has moved on constitutes retrodiction—what has already happened—and prediction—what is going to happen. We do not live out our whole horoscope all of the time and the movement of the chart shows how different factors will come into and go out of focus over the years.

There are two techniques for assessing the movement of the planets and angles: transits and progressions, and these are referred to as timing measures. Working with the progressed chart is covered in the following chapter.

LITERAL TRANSITS

There is no mathematics involved in working out transits, as they are taken straight from the ephemerides. You are simply looking for where the planets are on any given date, and comparing these to the position of the planets and angles in the birth chart. The astrologer then notes the aspects being formed from the transiting (moving) planets to the birth (stationary) planets. The slower-moving planets are the most important for transits—Jupiter, Saturn, Uranus, Neptune, and Pluto.

SYMBOLIC PROGRESSIONS

In the progressed chart, each day subsequent to the date of birth corre-sponds to each year of the native's life. For example, the 20th day after the date of birth would correlate to the native's 20th year. The position of the planets on the 20th day would show the position of the progressed planets, that is, how far they have moved on by progression. The fully progressed chart also shows how the angles have moved on. The astrologer then compares the progressed planets and angles to the nativity. The swifter-moving planets are the most important for progressions—the Sun, the Moon, Mercury, Venus, and Mars.

CYCLES AND RETURNS

Before working with progressions it is important to become proficient in the use of transits. The first step is to learn the cycles of the planets—how long they take to make a full orbit of the 12 signs—which were first mentioned in chapter two. The Sun travels through the 12 signs once a year and returns to its original position on our birthday. This is the Solar Return—many happy returns of the day—and all the planets have their own cycles, returns, quarter, or half returns.

WHY ARE FASTER PLANETS LESS IMPORTANT BY TRANSIT?

As each planet moves around the horoscope at its own speed it will transit—cross over—the other planets in the chart. The Sun will transit each of the nine other planets and the angles within the course of a year but, because the Sun moves so quickly, one degree a day, these transits last only for a day, and the same applies to Mercury and Venus. Mars has a two-year cycle, so Mars transits last for two days.

These contacts are therefore not significant in terms of major life events or changes but tend to operate at a more day-to-day level. For example, a Venus transit could be a special day, delicious food, a shopping trip, or a gift. A Mercury transit could be a decision, an idea, a phone call, an email, or an important conversation. A Mars transit could be an argument, a cut, a burst of energy, or passionate sex.

ONE OR THREE CONTACTS?

The slower-moving the planet, the longer that planet will take to travel over any given point. For example, the Sun transiting Pluto takes a day, but if it is the other way around—Pluto transiting the Sun—this transit will take about nine months. The slower-moving planets are therefore important by transit because they take a long time to move through each sign and they can stay on one degree for days or even weeks. Their transits rarely speak of isolated day-to-day events but of the unfolding of a particular

A Mars transit could signify an argument, a burst of energy, or passionate sex.

situation or relationship during the time that the transit lasts. The last three planets in particular—Uranus, Neptune, and Pluto—also spend long periods of time in retrograde motion. This means that they can spend months moving backward and forward over a particular degree, usually making three exact contacts. This can occasionally be true of Jupiter and Saturn transits as well.

Very occasionally a planet will make five transits. For the transits example in the box below, Neptune continues to move on after 15 July 1998 and then turns retrograde again in May 1999—but doesn't travel back as far as 1 degree of Aquarius. In this example,

---

TRANSITS EXAMPLE

Let us assume that we are looking at a natal chart in which the Sun is at 1 degree of Aquarius. (The Sun is simply an example, it could be any planet or angle.)

Looking back through the ephemerides you will find that Neptune entered Aquarius at the end of January 1998 and first reached 1 degree of Aquarius on 26 February 1998.

Moving forward through the ephemerides you will find that Neptune turns retrograde on 4 May 1998. This means that Neptune is moving backward through Aquarius from this date.

Continue moving forward through the ephemerides and you will see that Neptune gets back to 1 degree of Aquarius on 15 July 1998. This is its second contact.

Continue moving forward through the ephemerides and you will find that Neptune turns direct again on 11 October 1998. This means that Neptune is moving forward again from this date.

Continue moving forward through the ephemerides and you will find that Neptune gets back to 1 degree of Aquarius on 30 December 1998. This is the third and final contact.

---

we conclude that Neptune was transiting the Sun for ten months, from 26 February 1998 to 30 December 1998, with the middle retrograde contact falling on 15 July 1998. The first contact is likely to flag up the opening of a new chapter, often the middle retrograde contact will reveal the meaning and nature of the transit in question, producing some kind of turning point, and the third and final contact will bring an outcome or resolution. Sometimes you will find that events coincide with the exact dates of the transit but, mostly, you will find that key developments fall a few weeks either side of the exact dates.

Listing the dates of a planet's transits, as in the example in the box on the left, may look laborious, but the more you use the ephemerides, the more quickly you will familiarize yourself with the cycles of the planets. If you try to keep track of the planets in the present day, and you also know how fast they move, you will soon learn how to estimate an approximate date when looking for transits and returns, eliminating the need for time-consuming page-turning. For example, if I know that Uranus has just gone into Pisces on 15 April 2003, then I also know that Uranus was in Virgo about 40 years ago because Uranus has an approximately 80-year cycle, and Virgo is opposite Pisces in the horoscope, half-way in the cycle, and therefore represents half of the time period: 40 years. In this way I wouldn't need to look through every year of the ephemerides searching for Uranus in Virgo.

ASPECTS FORMED BY TRANSITING PLANETS

A planet transiting by conjunction—crossing the same degree and sign as in the example on the left—is, in my experience, the most powerful. However, planets transiting by opposition are also important, followed by squares and trines. The minor aspects need not be considered when working out transits.

THE PLANETS IN TRANSIT

When interpreting transits there are several factors to bear in mind:

- Universal symbolism—"opportunity" for Jupiter, "delays" for Saturn, "unexpected" for Uranus, etc.
- Particular symbolism—what is the natal condition of the transiting planet? Consider its house, sign, and aspect. Which house(s) does the transiting planet rule?
- What is the condition of the planet being transited? Consider its house, sign, aspects, and the house(s) that it rules.
- Consider the combination of the transiting and transited planets. For example, Saturn transiting Venus (romance, pleasure at a universal level, who or what in particular) will paint a different picture compared to Saturn transiting Mercury (communication, decisions at a universal level, who or what in particular).

These points are illustrated in the following section on the last five planets in transit. Also, bear in mind that if a planet is strongly placed in the nativity, it is more likely to be strong by transit as well. For example, if Jupiter is strongly placed then we would refer to the native as Jupiterian. Jupiterian types are more likely to have significant Jupiter transits and returns, Saturnian types are more likely to have significant Saturn transits and returns, and so on.

The best way to start learning about returns and transits is by looking at your own horoscope, simply because you know your own life better than anyone else's. Note where Jupiter is natally—its house and sign—and then note the houses that it rules. Then note from the ephemerides where Jupiter is now—is Jupiter crossing over any of your natal planets or angles? If not, when did you last experience a Jupiter transit or return? What happened? Can you see the events in terms of Jupiter's universal symbolism and/or in terms of what or who Jupiter rules in your chart? Can you see a showing of Jupiter symbolism combined with the symbolism of the other planet? If you do this exercise for all the planets from Jupiter to Pluto, you will quickly see how transits make your chart come to life, and you will also see how the symbolism of the different planets has manifested in your life. Picking out a relevant transit for somebody else—a friend, relative, or client—is especially exciting as that is generally the moment when astrology really starts to make sense and mean something.

JUPITER

Jupiter has a 12-year cycle so we experience our Jupiter returns at the ages of 12, 24, 36, and so on. Throughout that 12-year journey Jupiter will also transit the other nine planets and the angles. At a universal level we can expect events of a Jupiterian nature to unfold at these times. Remember that Jupiter is known as the Greater Benefic, so Jupiter contacts are generally good news, and they are mainly associated with education, travel, growth, and expansion of all kinds. The first Jupiter return at the age of 12 corresponds, in the Western world, to the beginning of secondary education and, often, the onset of puberty. In other cultures it may correspond to rituals designed to mark the transition from childhood into the adult world. Whatever the situation, Jupiter moves you on and makes your world a bigger place.

LUCKY OPPORTUNITY

At a particular level the planets' returns signal events that correspond to the role they play in each individual horoscope. For example, if there is a seventh house connection—Jupiter in the seventh house or ruling the seventh house—a Jupiter return is most likely to speak of relationship issues. Jupiter's symbolism of luck and opportunity could manifest as a new face coming into the picture, as good fortune for our partner, or as liberation from an unhappy relationship. The same could be said of Jupiter transiting the Descendant (the seventh-house cusp) and moving into the seventh house, or transiting planets in the seventh.

If Jupiter is in the tenth house or ruler of the tenth house, then a Jupiter return is most likely to speak of career issues, such as success in business, a new job, a promotion, or the opportunity to travel through work. The same can be said of Jupiter transiting the Midheaven (the tenth-house cusp) and moving into the tenth house, or transiting planets in the tenth. For one woman, Jupiter transiting Pluto in Virgo in the tenth house proved to be a liberation from an extremely difficult, over-controlling boss who had made her life a misery. Within one week of the Jupiter transit she was headhunted by a rival company and three weeks later she was working for someone who gave her freedom to do things in her own way.

SATURN THROUGH TO PLUTO

Every astrologer loves to see Jupiter in action because it stands for so many of the good things in life. Messages of good fortune, encouragement, and optimism are easy to pass on. But with Saturn through to Pluto we are dealing with planets that are traditionally malefic in nature. This means that they generally symbolize that which is testing, frustrating, difficult, or even tragic.

It is tempting to try and glamorize the transits of the outer planets but this needs to be resisted, especially when working with clients. There are often silver linings in the blackest of clouds, but sometimes there aren't. Even if there are they can take a long time to emerge, and in the meantime someone is having a hard time. This needs to be accepted and validated and I have always felt that it is important not to be a "good news" astrologer. You don't have to be overly pessimistic, but the last thing that someone wants to hear is that "everything's fine" when it clearly isn't. When we go through hard times, it is difficult to remember that they will not last forever and that things always change and move on. The astrologer's challenge is to communicate the message in a way that is real and meaningful for the client, and working with transits gives us the chance to do this. You will be amazed at the relief that is evident when you can locate a difficult event in a transit (and/or progression), describe its nature, and give the date when it finishes.

SATURN

Saturn has a 29½-year cycle so we experience our first Saturn return at this age, and the second in our late fifties. Anyone who lives to the age of 88 would experience a third Saturn return. Throughout its 29½-year journey Saturn will also transit the other nine planets and the angles. At a universal level we can expect events of a Saturnian nature to unfold at these times. Remember that Saturn is the Greater Malefic, so Saturn contacts are generally not good news. However, a lot depends on the condition of the natal Saturn, the houses it rules, and whether it is friend or foe to the native.

The first Saturn return is a notoriously difficult time, often referred to as the "astrological coming of age." Saturn is the Grim Reaper and in the months leading up to our 30th birthday it is a common experience to consider the thought of our own mortality—Saturn marks the ticking of the clock. Some may even experience a bereavement at this time. The positive side to this picture is that Saturn can speak of "getting it together" as we learn its qualities of hard work, self discipline, the readiness to accept extra responsibility, and setting goals. It is not uncommon for people to get married and settle down under the Saturn return.

By transit Saturn can signal tough times, especially if it is makes three contacts. If we are lucky it just makes one transit and moves on, but if there are three contacts we are in for a prolonged period of Saturnian issues. Saturn is a taskmaster so it may symbolize a time of especially hard work or times when we have to invest extra effort in order to get results. Saturn transits can also spell denial, delays, or disappointment, and I have seen many examples of this in relationships, such as meeting someone at the wrong time, unrequited love, or battling with a relationship that can never be what we want. Saturn

transits put the brakes on life, so they can also bring illness, forcing us out of the fast lane. As Saturn rules the teeth, look out for dental problems, too.

URANUS

Uranus has a 76–84-year cycle. It has an erratic orbit and is erratic by nature. You will come across Saturn on his second or even third trip around the horoscope but, because Uranus' cycle is slow, any transits from Uranus to the other planets or angles are "one-offs" and therefore score high on the scale of symbolic importance. As the Uranus return is not experienced until we are in our late seventies or early eighties, it is its halfway point that is particularly important. For example, if natal Uranus is at 4 degrees of Virgo then Uranus will have reached its halfway point when it arrives at 4 degrees of Pisces. The Uranus half return falls anywhere between the 38th and 42nd birthday.

SUDDEN SHOCKS

If the Saturn return is our astrological coming of age, then the Uranus half return is our astrological mid-life crisis. In the words of astrologer Liz Greene, "the opposition of Uranus to its natal place symbolizes the release of that which has been unlived with powerful force." That which has been neglected or repressed is most likely to struggle to the surface at this time. And as Uranus symbolizes change, shock, rebellion, and innovation, the results can bring anything from exciting developments to chaos and disruption.

Typical Uranus half return events turn a person's life on its head, the ultimate being tales of rags to riches or riches to rags. But often it is more a case of breaking the mold that has been cast in the first half

of life. For instance, those who have diligently followed a career could make startling progress, or quit
and set off to do something different. Those who have
been married for years split up or have affairs. Those
who have raised a family and see children leaving
home suddenly find their role in life dramatically
altered. Some experience this as the empty nest syn-
drome, others will embrace new-found freedom,
others, who have "hidden" behind children or stayed
in a marriage because of children, may go through a
considerable period of disintegration before finding a
way in which to regroup. Conversely, some may have a
"last chance" baby before fertility disappears, and
those who have never been married suddenly meet
someone and tie the knot; those who have never
traveled get itchy feet, those who lacked an education
go back to college, and so on.

At a universal level Uranus in transit signals that
which is unexpected, often something you couldn't
have seen coming. Things go haywire, and there is a
feeling of being out of control, of life being upside
down and back to front. Even something that is
expected can work out in an unforeseen way. As you
might imagine, it is tricky for the astrologer to make
any predictions when Uranus is in the picture. But, as
always, look at the natal condition of Uranus and
matters pertaining to its role in the individual
horoscope. Always look for the house that it co-rules—
that is, the house with Aquarius on the cusp—and
consider the condition of the planet being transited.

The astrologer Maggie Hyde first alerted me to the
interesting irony of Uranus transits. For all its
unpredictability, Uranus transits often work out to
exactitude in terms of dates, and I have seen this on
more than one occasion.

A TRAUMATIC YEAR

For example, a horoscope for a woman born in 1959
gives 15 degrees of Capricorn rising, so her

A Uranus half-return can manifest in splitting up or divorce.

Descendant is 15 degrees of Cancer. Venus, at just over
16 degrees of Cancer, is conjunct the Descendant.
Uranus is in the seventh house at 12.45 degrees of
Leo. When she came to see me in early 1993,
transiting Uranus was at 18 degrees of Capricorn. She
was yet to experience the Uranus half return, which
would occur when Uranus reached 12.45 of Aquarius,
but I was able to give her the dates for when Uranus
had crossed her Ascendant—and so opposed her
Descendant—and thus also opposed Venus
throughout 1992. She was astonished when I gave her
the last date in this series of contacts: Uranus' final
opposition to Venus. All the transits accurately framed
and described a year of emotional trauma, near
bankruptcy, and disruption at every level, and it
turned out that the final transit date was the day that
her husband had walked out into the arms of another
woman, never to return.

You may wonder if Uranus always signals heavy drama, and it is true that the outer planets do tend to speak of life's difficulties rather than pleasures. However, recently I had an example of Uranus as a wonderful surprise. In this man's horoscope Mars was at 0 degrees of Pisces in the second house. Uranus had just entered Pisces, at the time of the reading, so had made its first transit across Mars. Aquarius was on the 11th cusp, so Uranus was the co-ruler of the house of friends. On the day that Uranus reached Mars the man's friend (Uranus co-ruling the 11th house) won some money (Mars in the second house) on the lottery (the suddenness of Uranus) and invited him on holiday (the friend's sudden luck being shared with him). I had yet to see what the rest of year would

bring as Uranus would make another two contacts to Mars but, if the first showing was anything to go by, it didn't look as if he had too much to worry about.

NEPTUNE

Neptune has an approximately 170-year orbit so even a half return doesn't occur until we're 85 years old. The only return worth noting for Neptune is the quarter return when we are in our early forties.

By transit Neptune is, in my experience, one of the most difficult planets to contend with. If Saturn imposes discipline or restriction, and Uranus pulls the rug from under our feet, then Neptune distorts, dissolves, and deludes. It is god of the sea and under Neptune's mists and fogs confusion reigns and

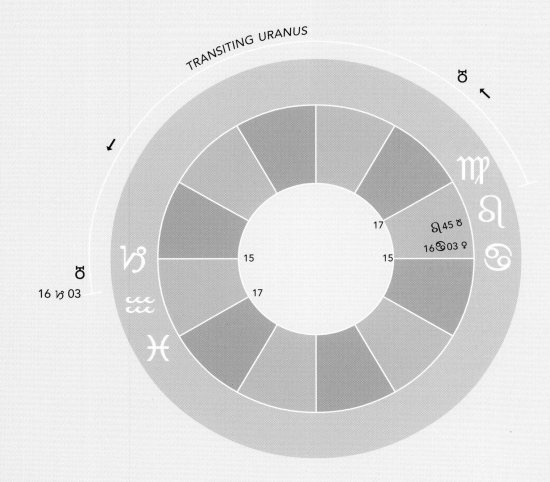

Neptune transits can find us lost at sea in a fog of confusion.

able to work out why, not knowing where to turn or what to do for the best. Quite often the only advice the astrologer can offer is to "go with the flow."

ROSE-TINTED ROMANCE

Relationships that come together under Neptune can initially be the stuff of fairytales. With rose-tinted spectacles firmly in place, we idealize, our personal boundaries collapse, we crave fusion—the urge to merge, and escapism looms large. A classic example of this was the marriage of Prince Charles to Diana. Natally, Prince Charles has a Venus-Neptune conjunction in Libra, Diana had a Sun-Mercury conjunction in Cancer, trine Neptune in Scorpio, and Neptune was active in her chart at the time of the wedding. The whole world was entranced with the image, not knowing that it was a Neptunian illusion and that the bubble would burst tragically.

With Neptune's connection to sensitive Pisces and the 12th house, the vale of tears and sacrifice, Neptune transits can signify times of suffering and emotional distress for which keywords such as "confusion" are inadequate. Neptune issues speak of soul searching, with connections to moral dilemmas, personal sacrifices, conscience, or guilt. For one woman a Neptune transit across the Moon related to a deeply regretted abortion. For a man in his mid-forties a Neptune transit over Venus spoke of a long period of agonizing over whether or not to leave a needy partner. The astrologer knows that, whatever the issue, things happen for a reason but, when Neptune is in the picture, that reason is likely to be obscure.

PLUTO

Pluto is the slowest-moving planet of all, with a cycle of 248 years. Even a quarter return would not happen until we are over 60, so this planet is at its most important when transiting the other planets or angles. By transit Pluto often symbolizes total change through

nothing is clear-cut. We are all at sea, cut adrift, no longer sure of what is fact or fantasy. Situations or events that unfold under Neptune transits are either disorienting, painful, or impossible to understand, often because we are out of control or out of the picture. For one woman, a Neptune transit over Mercury related to the time when her family concealed from her the truth of her mother's terminal illness and she was unable to get a straight answer to a straight question. The general backdrop to Neptune transits is a sense of nothing going right but not being a symbolic death and rebirth. One of the most popular keywords for Pluto is "transformation," but this word needs to be used carefully as it can fall drastically short of describing the Plutonic experience. "Transformation" tends to suggest change that is rapid, but Pluto transits generally last about nine months, a gestation period, and the symbolic death and rebirth is always a process of change, not an overnight sensation. Furthermore, Pluto is the god of the underworld and Pluto transits can, at their worst, be a trip to hell and back as one way of life "dies" in order for a new one to be born. A more accurate keyword for Pluto is "uncompromising."

For a woman in her early forties Pluto transiting Venus, her ruling planet, was the time when she left her husband. Because she was intimidated by him she simply went away and didn't go back, living out Pluto's symbolism of disappearance, absence, or invisibility. She spent the ensuing 18 months in poverty while she slowly rebuilt her life. She rose from the ashes but not without considerable trauma and physical hardship.

For another woman life changed when Pluto transited her Sun when she was a teenager. Often the Sun signifies the father, especially in a woman's horoscope, and at this time her father had a heart attack and was unable to return to work. The family moved to a quiet village, a disastrous event for a growing girl who had to leave her friends, school, and plans behind her. She feels her life would have been very different if she had not been uprooted at this crucial age.

HEALING POTENTIAL

However, not all Pluto contacts work at such a dramatic level. Life is never the same again after Pluto but there is also a healing potential within this planet. When I talked to one woman about the time Pluto had transited her Ascendant—the physical body—she told me that it was at this time that she had discovered Prozac. After years of depression and seeing therapists she resorted to a medical remedy that, for her, resulted in transformation.

Finally, Pluto is associated with wealth, as explained in chapter two, but examples of Pluto transits bringing prosperity are, in my experience, rare. However, because of Pluto's dominion of the eighth house—the house of death—money may come as an inheritance.

Pluto transits often involve a symbolic death and rebirth.

LUNATIONS

Lunations—also called syzygies—are either new or full Moons and are an expression of the relationship between the lights—the Sun and the Moon. As the Moon has a 28-day cycle, there is a new Moon or full Moon every 14 days.

NEW MOON

This is when the Moon is exactly conjunct the Sun, so the lights are therefore always in the same sign. For this reason the exact new Moon is invisible as it cannot receive any of the Sun's light. When we first see the sliver of the new Moon in the sky this is actually two to three days after the exact new Moon. This two- to three-day period when there is no Moon is called the Dark of the Moon, considered to be unlucky or malefic as it is associated with black magic.

FULL MOON

This is when the Moon is exactly opposite the Sun, so the lights are therefore always in opposite signs. At this time the whole face of the Moon receives the light of the Sun and is totally visible in the sky.

NEW MOON

The 14 days from the new Moon to the next full Moon is when the Moon is waxing, or getting bigger and stronger. The new Moon marks the opening of a new cycle and is associated with beginnings, fertility, and development. This is a time for sowing seeds and making fresh starts.

FULL MOON

The 14 days from the full Moon to the next new Moon is when the Moon is waning, or getting weaker. The full Moon marks the completion of a cycle and is associated with recognition, achievement, fulfillment, and illumination. There is a sense of heightened energy, of things being at either full power or at full stretch, so a full Moon can be positive or negative depending on what is unleashed. It is the full Moon that is associated with both "lunacy" and white magic.

In terms of particular symbolism, lunations are important if they fall on a sensitive degree of the horoscope. In other words, if a lunation falls in the same sign and within a couple of degrees of a natal planet or angle, then that lunation would be considered significant for the native. However, it is rare for a lunation to signify noteworthy events simply in its own right. More often than not a lunation will act as a testimony to judgment, that is, confirmation and reinforcement of a pattern that is already showing itself through transits and progressions.

In terms of prediction, lunations are especially helpful. Transits and progressions can be in operation for many months at a time and a lunation can often pinpoint a two-week period that is especially sensitive. For example, if transits and/or progressions suggest that a new relationship is on the horizon, then a new or full Moon falling on the Ascendant or Descendant, on planets in the seventh house or ruler of the seventh, or maybe Venus or Mars as universal signifiers of romance, can narrow down the time scale from months or weeks to a couple of weeks or even days.

With the Moon's connection to women and fertility I have found that lunations are especially powerful when it comes to the astrology of conception, pregnancy, and birth. For example, for one woman the natal promise of children was strong—her ruling planet Mercury conjunct the Sun in the fifth house (children)—and on the birth of her first child in February 1988 there was a power-ful line up of transits and pro-gressions that involved her fifth-house planets and Venus—who also features strongly in relation to children and motherhood. Com-pleting the picture was a new Moon at 28 Capricorn exactly conjunct her fifth-house cusp just over two weeks before the birth, followed by a full Moon at 13 Leo opposite her fifth house planets within three days of the birth.

LUNAR AND SOLAR RETURNS

We tend to think of there being one new and full Moon every month but, with a 28-day cycle, there are in fact 13 of each throughout the year. This also means that, in the nativity, the Moon will return to its natal position 13 times in any 12-month period. The moment when the Moon returns to its natal position is called the Lunar Return and, if you cast a horoscope for that exact moment, this yields the Lunar Return horoscope, which is said to paint the picture for the ensuing 28 days. You can think of the Lunar Return chart as "flavor of the month." However, these horoscopes should not be given too much importance as it is true to say that some Lunar Return charts work better than others. Adding this predictive string to your bow is a rather hit-and-miss affair.

The Solar Return horoscope is cast for the moment when the Sun returns to its exact natal position and is valid for the ensuing 12 months. Similarly, this chart is said to speak of the year ahead but, again, some work better than others. I personally do not cast Lunar or Solar Return horoscopes for clients, but I do my own, treating them as an interesting exercise. The calculation of these charts involves a rather lengthy and complicated use of logarithms—which are not within the scope of this book—so it is useful to have computer software to help with this.

ECLIPSES

Eclipses occur when a new or full Moon is also conjunct the Moon's nodes—the imaginary points at which the Moon cuts across the Ecliptic. Eclipses can be partial or total, the latter considered to be the most potent in terms of astrological symbolism.

Solar Eclipse—This occurs when the Sun is obscured by the shadow of the Moon at the time of a new Moon.

Lunar Eclipse—This occurs when the Moon is obscured by the shadow of the Earth at the time of a full Moon.

Solar eclipses occur between two to five times a year, whereas lunar eclipses occur once or twice a year. In the ephemerides you will find the date, type, degree, and time of any eclipses listed separately at the top of the page.

WHAT DO ECLIPSES SYMBOLIZE?

There are two schools of thought for interpreting eclipses. One considers them to be bad news, as eclipse images point to such symbolism as a light going out, the throwing of shadows, or a loss of power. There is also a flavor of death and rebirth symbolism—the light disappearing and coming back again. In this respect, eclipses fall more into the category of omens—unbidden phenomena that signal change in the life of an individual or a nation.

The other interpretation sees eclipses—like lunations—as powerful testimonies to transits, or to natal or progressed configurations. This latter school of thought is expounded in *Eclipses—the Power Points of Astrology* by Derek Appleby and Maurice McCann. The main thesis is that eclipses are not just portents of disaster—although they can be—but that they "sensitize" when they fall—by conjunction, opposition or square—on an individual's or nation's natal or progressed planets or angles. In this book you will find numerous fascinating examples of eclipses in action, including the abdication of Edward VIII in relation to the horoscope of his brother, George VI, who had kingship thrust upon him.

A SOLAR ECLIPSE

◆ Edward VIII abdicated on 10 December 1936.

◆ A solar eclipse fell at 21.49 Sagittarius just three days later, on 13 December 1936.

◆ His brother George VI was born on 14 December, with his natal Sun at 21.55 Sagittarius, almost exactly conjunct the eclipse degree.

The astrological symbolism of this eclipse is radical—it paints a powerfully accurate picture of the event in question. Not only is George VI's Sun conjunct the eclipse degree, his Sun in his natal chart is conjunct the third cusp—the house of siblings. Furthermore, his Sun in Sagittarius rules his Leo Midheaven (status) and is in mutual reception (when two planets are in each other's signs) with Jupiter in Leo, which is conjunct his Midheaven—in itself a fitting symbolic picture for a man who is to be a monarch. The eclipse falling conjunct his Sun on the third-house cusp sensitizes the natal configuration. His brother is eclipsed, and in fact spent the rest of his life in exile, the mutual reception between the Sun and Jupiter is made, and George is crowned in Edward's place. Note also that, at the time of the abdication, Pluto was in the middle of a long transit over Edward's Mercury—a final and irrevocable decision.

A LUNAR ECLIPSE

Many astrologers have written about the horoscope of Diana, the Princess of Wales. Two horoscopes exist for Diana because two different birth times were given for her. In *The Moment of Astrology*, Geoffrey Cornelius discusses both charts, particularly regarding the phenomenon of the "wrong" chart working, and shows how a case can be made for either chart. Part of his thesis for the second horoscope is the occurrence of a lunar eclipse.

◆ On 9 December the Prime Minister announced in the House of Commons the formal separation of the Prince and Princess of Wales.

- On the same day there was a total eclipse of the Moon at 18.10 Gemini.
- The supposedly corrected birth time for Diana—from the original 2.00 pm to 7.45 pm—gives an Ascendant of 18.24 Sagittarius. So the eclipse fell almost exactly conjunct her Descendant, the marriage angle of the chart, of 18.24 Gemini.

The eclipse clearly symbolized the end of the marriage but, more importantly, at the time of the announcement the Prime Minister stated that Diana's role as Queen if Charles became King was not in question. But, as Geoffrey Cornelius points out, astrologers knew better:

"...that very night everyone with even a grain of symbolism had a more immediate and dramatic celestial indication of the true state of affairs...the Sun and Moon in opposition, the King and the Queen, but with the shadow of the world between them. The noble Diana, like her namesake the Moon, enthroned at the Midheaven yet darkened. How could she now be Queen?"

These two royal stories—Edward's abdication and George's succession, the destruction of Diana's marriage and status—are perfect showings of eclipse symbolism. More importantly, they delineate the relevant events with stunning simplicity. Whether you are looking at natal charts, transits or progressions, or lunations or eclipses, the hallmark of radical astrology—that is, horoscopes that yield accurate and unmistakable symbolism—is simplicity. As with the above stories, such simplicity is revealed through the careful application of astrological craft, allowing the horoscope to speak its own individual symbolism.

In this total solar eclipse the black circle of the Moon covers the disc of the Sun.

As the name suggests, progressions show how the chart moves on, month by month, year by year. Rather than relating to the cycles of the planets, as transits do, progressions constitute a symbolic timing measure that reveals and maps the major life events of each individual. The progressed horoscope is the most important string to the astrologer's bow, either when looking back into the past or forward into the future. This chapter introduces the basic calculations and illustrates how to identify, prioritize, and interpret the progressions for different events.

LOCATING PROGRESSIONS

WORKING WITH PROGRESSIONS

Transits can be highly descriptive, and sometimes they do speak of events single-handedly, but often they are a testimony to the bigger picture, boasting their true power when working hand in hand with progressions.

Once you have mastered using the ephemerides you will find that you are able to locate transits quickly. Learning to use transits is such an interesting stage for the developing astrologer that it can be tempting to stay in this "safety zone," but transits alone are only part of the picture. Transits become even more interesting when they are combined with progressions.

WHAT ARE PROGRESSIONS?

As stated in the previous chapter, progressions are a symbolic timing measure. Every day subsequent to the date of birth represents a year in the native's life so, for example, the tenth day after the date of birth corresponds to the beginning of the tenth year of life. This explains why the faster-moving planets are more important in progressions as, by progression—day to day—they move quite quickly. For example, Mercury when moving at full speed can progress through two, three, or four complete signs for someone who lives into his or her seventies, making aspects to the other planets as it moves on, and the aspects it makes are called progressions. By comparison, the slower-moving planets can stay on the same degree for weeks at a time, which translates into years at a time in progressions. It is therefore rare for a slow-moving planet to make a progression,

"Study the past, if you would divine the future."

Confucius

that is, to be the applying planet, the one that is moving in order to make an aspect with a second planet.

Having isolated a given date, the astrologer then looks at the position of the progressed planets. If any of the progressed planets are at the same degree (of any sign) as any of the natal planets or angles, this signals a progression. When the progressed planet is at the same degree and minute as any of the natal planets or angles, the progression will be exact. If a progressed planet is at the same degree as any of the natal planets or angles, this is called progressed to natal. If any of the progressed planets hold the same degree, this is called progressed to progressed. The initial "p" after a planet indicates that you are referring to its progressed position.

PROGRESSED TO NATAL

If a progressed planet is in any aspect to any natal planet or angle this is called a progression. Always state the applying planet—the one making the aspect— first. For example, if the natal Sun is at 5 Aries and the progressed Mars is at 5 Aries this is stated as: Mars p conjunct the Sun. ♂p☌☉

PROGRESSED TO PROGRESSED

If the progressed planets make any aspects between themselves, irrespective of the natal planets, these are also called progressions. Always state the faster-moving planet first. For example, if the progressed Sun is at 5 Aries and the progressed Mars is at 5 Aries this would be stated as: Sun p conjunct Mars p. ☉p☌♂p

When I first started studying progressions I assumed that progressed to natal were the most important. However, when I couldn't find progressions for certain events in progressed to natal, I would always find my answers in progressed to progressed.

UNDERSTANDING PROGRESSIONS

Becoming proficient in the use of progressions takes time and study and this department of astrology cannot be rushed. Many students feel anxious when they are introduced to the mathematics involved and give up on astrology at this stage, declaring that it is beyond them. Even those who have grasped the other technicalities may glaze over when they start trying to locate progressions, especially in terms of pinpointing those that are important and relevant.

Part of the confusion centers around not being confident with how progressions work at a technical level. Trying to work with progressions, both locating and interpreting them, without understanding the nuts and bolts involved, is nearly always a case of trying to run before you can walk. Secondly, it is often forgotten that progressions are an extension and confirmation of the natal chart. Whatever is indicated in the natal chart—the natal promise—will come to pass under relevant timing measures. In other words, both transits and progressions are an amplification of the natal chart because they "activate" the chart, but they can never change or override natal factors.

COMPUTER SOFTWARE

Computer software can be more and less useful regarding calculating progressions. Some packages simply give a list of every major and minor progression within a one-degree orb for any given date, but with no indication of an exact date. This is useless for the beginner as some progressions can be within a one-degree orb for years, and it is only the year of "perfection"—when a progression is exact—that will be relevant. Other packages give dates for exact progressions but with no distinction in terms of importance and priority. If you are unfamiliar with the mathematical machinery behind these calculations, it is impossible to sift through them, finding which ones are important and which are irrelevant. Software cannot interpret or sort the wheat from the chaff. This is a skill that the astrologer acquires only through assiduous study, and only then will a horoscope come fully alive for you. It is probably the biggest challenge when it comes to moving from being an average astrologer to being excellent.

The figures involved may look complicated, but the joy of astrological calculations is that, once you have learned a formula, you simply apply it over and over again. You do not have to learn a new set of rules for every chart. You can compare it with learning how to calculate a natal horoscope. At first it is a confusing maze, but it soon becomes a procedure with a definite pattern.

FIRST PRINCIPLES

It is a simplification to say that every day subsequent to the date of birth corresponds to a year of life. More

precisely, it is every day starting at exactly the same time of birth that corresponds to the beginning of each year. For example, if you were born at 18.00 on 1 January 1960 then the position of the planets at 18.00 on 11 January 1960 are the progressed planets for the beginning of the tenth year of life. I cannot turn to 11 January and read off the position of the planets on that day because those are the positions of the planets at midnight—0 hours—so I would be 18 hours adrift. When working with progressions you are always converting clock time—hours and minutes—into calendar time—days, weeks, and months. This is explained fully in the following section—the ACD—but for now note that 18 hours in progressions converts to nine months, a wide margin of error. So, how does the astrologer get around this mathematical challenge?

ADJUSTED CALCULATION DATE (ACD)

Rather than calculating the position of the planets for the same birth time whenever you want to look at a day (a year) of progressions, there is a shortcut that allows you always to work with the planets at midnight, as already listed in the ephemerides. This means that you do not have to keep doing sums. A one-off calculation for each chart is all that is required.

Planetary positions in the ephemerides are given for midnight—0h—or for midday—12h. All the calculations in this book are based on 0h positions. If someone is born at exactly midnight then you would read off the position of the planets for any date to see how far they had progressed—moved on in symbolic terms—for any year. However, as it is rare to be born at exactly midnight, how do you know when each person's "year" begins? The starting point is to make an adjustment that allows the astrologer to calculate a new "birthday," as the following procedure demonstrates.

Throughout this chapter I will use an example horoscope for Emma, born 5 April 1957 at 18.00, at 53N19, 2W57.

GMT

As with all astrological calculations the first rule is to get back to GMT. In 1957, British Summertime started on 14 April so the birth time of 18.00 is already in GMT, and no adjustment needs to be made.

A DAY EQUALS A YEAR

The most important concept when working with progressions is that, if a day equals a year, then 24 hours equal 12 months. If you continue to reduce this equation you will find that:

12 hours = 6 months

6 hours = 3 months

4 hours = 2 months

2 hours = 1 month

1 hour = 2 weeks

half an hour = 1 week

quarter of an hour = 3 days

TIME TO GO

How much time is there to go between the time of birth and the next midnight? Emma was born at 18.00 so there are six hours to go to the next midnight (0h).

Conversion Convert the hours and minutes of "the time to go"—not the time of birth—into months, weeks, and days. Six hours = three months.

Add to the date of birth Add the answer to the birth date. 5 April 1957 + three months = 5 July 1957. This is Emma's ACD. Her new "birthday" is 5 July 1957.

The day after The next midnight (0h) corresponds to 5 July 1957. This means that the position of the planets at 0h on 6 April 1957—the day after her birthday—are the progressed planets for her year beginning 5 July 1957.

This technique eliminates the need to calculate the planets for the time of birth for every set of progressions. The astrologer can now work straight from the 0h positions of the planets in the ephemerides for any year.

ACD SCHEDULE

You can now work ahead to any year by adding dates on one side and years on the other. Always write out your first line at the top of the page and then add to either side. It is always worth double-checking your first line before going any further because, if it is wrong, then the rest of the schedule will be wrong. If I accidentally wrote out the first line as 5 April 1957, her birth date, instead of the next day, my whole schedule would be out by a year.

ACD (0h) 6 April 1957 = 5 July 1957

(+ 1 day) 7 April 1957 = 5 July 1958 (+ 1 year)

8 April 1957 = 5 July 1959

9 April 1957 = 5 July 1960

10 April 1957 = 5 July 1961

11 April 1957 = 5 July 1962

12 April 1957 = 5 July 1963

13 April 1957 = 5 July 1964, and so on.

PROGRESSIONS FOR KEY DATES

There are two ways to use progressions: seeing which progressions are in operation at the time of a consultation or for key dates that a client gives you, or seeing when certain progressions perfected, or will perfect.

Working with past progressions first is vital because only by seeing how the progressed chart has already behaved can you confirm your natal interpretations.

I will look at a key date in Emma's chart: September 1968 when she was 11 years old. I therefore need to find the day that gives the progressed planets for her year beginning 5 July 1968. You do not need to write out every line to find the day that corresponds to the year that you want. Just make sure to always add one day on the left and one year on the right:

ACD (0h) 6 April 1957
= 5 July 1957
(+ 11 Days) 17 April 1957
= 5 July 1968 (+ 11 Years)

The position of the planets at 0h on 17 April 1957 is the progressed planets for her year beginning 5 July 1968.

HOW TO SPOT PROGRESSIONS

In time you will be able to spot progressions as easily as transits, but this comes with practice. While learning to use progressions the best technique is to lay out information pictorially. This may be labor intensive at first but it is fail-safe.

Line 1: Position of natal planets Take some squared paper and write the degrees 0–30 along the top. Then write the planets, the Ascendant (A) and Midheaven (M), and the Part of Fortune and the Moon's north node underneath their degree number, rounding up to the next degree where appropriate. For example, Emma's natal Moon is at 18.59 Gemini, so it is placed under 19 degrees.

Line 2: Position of progressed planets
Using your previous calculations, write the progressed planets below: the position of the planets at 0h on 17 April 1957 (= year beginning 5 July 1968). You can see how the progressed planets line up with the natal planets, and how the progressed planets are positioned in relation to each other. I have also included the progressed angles but will explain these later.

Line 3: Progressions for this year Firstly, are any progressed planets and natal planets at the same degree? If the progressed planet is slow-moving, I note the progression as possible. Working from left to right across line 3:

- Neptune is still at 1 degree of Scorpio, so check to see if it is opposite natal Mercury in Taurus. Possible progression: Neptune progressed to oppose Mercury. Ψp☍☿

- Saturn in Sagittarius is retrograde and at 13 degrees, the same degree as natal Venus in Aries. Possible progression: Saturn progressed to trine Venus. ♄p△♀

- The progressed Ascendant in Libra is at the same degree as the Sun in Aries. These are opposite signs. Progression: Ascendant progressed to oppose the Sun. Ascp☍☉

- Mars is at 18 degrees of Gemini, nearing the degree and sign of the natal Moon. Possible progression: Mars progressed to conjunct the Moon. ♂p♂☽

- Venus is at 27 degrees of Aries, approaching the same degree as Pluto in Leo. Possible progression: Venus progressed to trine Pluto. ♀p△♇

Secondly, do any of the progressed planets hold the same degree?

- The Sun has reached 26 degrees of Aries and Venus has reached 27 degrees of Aries. The Sun and Venus are next to each other in the same sign. Possible progression: progressed Sun conjunct progressed Venus. ☉p♂♀p

- Progressed Pluto, the slowest-moving planet, is still at the same degree as in the natal chart. We have already identified Venus progressed to trine Pluto.

We must also check progressed Venus trine progressed Pluto. ♀p△♇p

A NOTE ON ASPECTS

The aspects between the natal planets play a vital role in interpretation. However, the aspects formed by progressions are less critical. The major aspects are most important and the aspect formed may be symbolically appropriate—such as a square or an opposition for difficulties—but this is not an infallible rule. It is often just as important to consider the nature of the two planets united by progression as to focus on the aspect. In Emma's chart for 5 July 1968, progressed Venus trines progressed Pluto. The trine—a benefic aspect—does not override the difficulties symbolized by Pluto.

PROGRESSIONS DIAGRAM FOR EMMA

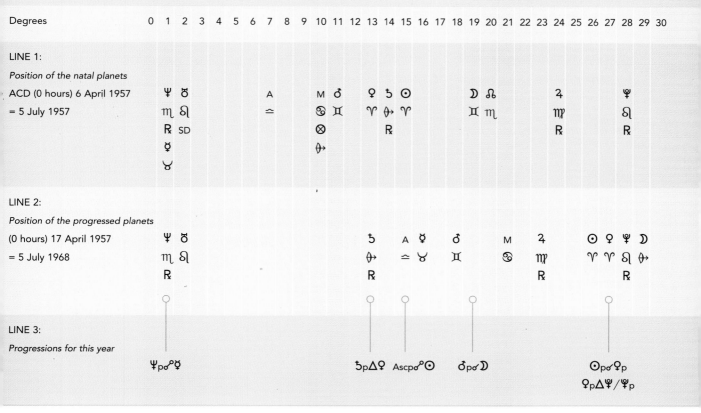

Degrees	0 1 2 3 4 5 6 7 8 9 10 11 12 13 14 15 16 17 18 19 20 21 22 23 24 25 26 27 28 29 30

LINE 1:
Position of the natal planets
ACD (0 hours) 6 April 1957
= 5 July 1957

LINE 2:
Position of the progressed planets
(0 hours) 17 April 1957
= 5 July 1968

LINE 3:
Progressions for this year

♇p♂♀   ♄p△♀ Ascp♂☉   ♂p♂☽   ☉p♂♀p
                                      ♀p△♇/♇p

THE LENGTH OF PROGRESSIONS

There are varying opinions as to quantifying the lifetime of progressions because they do not usually coincide precisely with the date when they become exact. This is because progressions generally describe a period of time in the native's life, the unfolding of events and circumstances, the preparation of conditions, and scenarios that will prove to be significant.

Some schools of thought say that a progression is potent for six months either side of its date of perfection—or exactitude—while others say that it is the previous year that is important. Some say that solar progressions—those made by the progressed Sun—have a longer lifetime than progressions that are made by the other planets.

Invariably the best guidelines are empirical, that is, those that are tried and tested, and especially those that arise from your own practice and observations. In my own experience I have found that a progression mostly comes to life anywhere in the three-month period before it is exact and that it can stay potent for up to two or sometimes three months after it is exact. However, progressions that are applying—becoming exact—are nearly always more powerful than those which are separating—have already happened. You can think of separating progressions as those that are past their "sell-by" date. Once you have located a progression, the next step is to find out when it is exact, and there are some simple calculations for getting you there.

WHEN IS A PROGRESSION EXACT?

Let's go back to Emma's progressions diagram and the events at age 11 (see page 117). We have already completed the diagram for the planets on 17 April 1957 (= year beginning 5 July 1968), which isolates the possible progressions at this time. Not counting, for now, the progressed Ascendant opposing the Sun, which I will cover later, there are six possible progressions to investigate. Working across the progressions from left to right on the diagram these are:

Neptune p opposite Mercury

Saturn p trine Venus

Mars p conjunct Moon

Sun p conjunct Venus p
Venus p trine Pluto
Venus p trine Pluto p

The following calculations show how to date the individual progressions. I will take them in the same order as above, followed by the story of events in Emma's life at this time that supply the interpretation.

NEPTUNE PROGRESSED TO OPPOSE MERCURY

The slower-moving the planet, the more rare the possibility of it being the applying planet in a progression—that is, the planet that moves to make an aspect with another planet or angle. Furthermore, a progression made by a slow-moving planet can happen only when that planet is already in a tight aspect to another in the natal chart, and that progression can appear to be in operation for years at a time. However, it is only the time when the progression is exact that is important, otherwise you would be taking it into account for literally years. The message is to tread carefully when working with the slower-moving planets.

Look at Emma's chart again and you will see that she has a fixed T-square—Mercury in Taurus opposite Neptune in Scorpio, both square to Uranus in Leo in the tenth house. This is a very tight T-square, as the orbs are small. In particular, Mercury at 1.21 Taurus opposite Neptune at 1.39 Scorpio are only 18 minutes of arc apart. Note that Neptune is retrograde, moving backward, so by progression, this opposition will perfect—become exact. In

other words, it is quite likely that Neptune, as long as it continues in retrograde motion, will progress back as far as 1.21 Scorpio, and will therefore end up being exactly opposite Mercury at 1.21 Taurus.

Looking in the ephemerides you will see that Neptune is at 1.22 Scorpio at 0h on 17 April (= 5 July 1968) and at 1.20 Scorpio at 0h on 18 April (= 5 July 1969). Note that Neptune is retrograde and therefore moving backward. Moving only two minutes of arc within this 24-hour period, Neptune therefore reaches 1.21 Scorpio, exactly opposing Mercury, halfway through the day. Twelve hours = six months, so add six months to the first corresponding date of 5 July 1968 and you arrive at 5 January 1969. Progressed Neptune is therefore exactly opposite Mercury on this date.

Is this progression relevant? Yes. This progression is exact four months after the date in question, September 1968, so this makes it an applying progression—yet to happen. Being a progression made by an outer planet makes it even more important, and when you read the following story you will see how the progression fits the experiences to come for Emma in the months following September 1968.

SATURN PROGRESSED TO TRINE VENUS

Here is the second example of a slow-moving planet being in tight aspect to another planet in the natal chart. Venus at 13.25 Aries is trine Saturn at 14.10 Sagittarius, so they are less than one degree apart. As with the previous example, this aspect is therefore likely to perfect by progression, especially as Saturn is retrograde—that is, moving backward and therefore gradually moving closer to the same degree and same minute as Venus.

Looking in the ephemerides on 17 April you will see that Saturn is still retrograde but has only moved backward as far as 13.50 Sagittarius. This means that the trine to Venus has not yet happened because at this time Saturn has still not traveled as far back as 13 degrees and 25 minutes of Sagittarius. If you look further ahead you will see that Saturn does not reach 13.25 of Sagittarius until 26 April, which corresponds to July 1977.

Is it relevant? No. You need to go no further in terms of finding the exact date for Saturn progressed to trine Venus. As this progression doesn't actually perfect until 1977, nearly nine years after the date in question, it is most definitely not relevant for now. This is a classic example of how a progression can appear to be in operation but in actual fact still has a long way to go.

MARS PROGRESSED TO CONJUNCT MOON

This step-by-step technique can be followed for dating any progressions to natal planets or angles.

◆ When is the applying planet at the same degree and minute as the natal planet?
Find out when progressed Mars reached 18.59 Gemini—exactly the same position as the natal Moon. Locate the two dates in the ephemerides that encompass this position: 0h 17 April 1957 (= 5 July 1968)—Mars is at 18.55 Gemini.
0h 18 April 1957 (= 5 July 1969)—Mars has reached 19.33 Gemini.

◆ What is the daily motion?
See how far the applying planet has moved in 24 hours. Mars has moved from 18♊55 to 19♊33, so the daily motion is 38 minutes of arc.

◆ What is the arc?
Find out the distance between the progressed planet at the first 0h position to the natal planet. What is the distance between Mars at 18♊55 to the natal Moon at 18♊59? In this example, progressed Mars has to move only 4 minutes of arc to reach the same position as the natal Moon.

◆ The formula
The unchanging formula for these calculations is the arc divided by the daily motion, multiplied by 12 (months in a year). So, 4 divided by 38 multiplied by 12 = 1.26. This is not one month and 26 days but one month and 0.26 of a month, which is 8 days. The answer then is 1 month and 8 days.

◆ The answer
Add your answer to the first 0h date of 5 July 1968, so the final answer is 13 August 1968. This is when

progressed Mars is exactly conjunct the natal Moon in Emma's chart.

Is it relevant? Yes. Looking at the progressed picture for September 1968, I can take this as a key progression as it is only just separating, being exact only a month before the date in question.

SUN PROGRESSED TO CONJUNCT PROGRESSED VENUS

In order to date progressed to progressed contacts you will need an ephemerides that includes an aspectarian. This is a table at the bottom of each page that lists the aspects for each day. It will tell you which planets are in aspect, what kind of aspect is being formed, and at what time the aspect is exact. It also gives exact times for ingresses—when a planet changes sign—or for when a planet turns retrograde or direct.

This step-by-step technique can be followed for dating any progressed to progressed contacts.

- Locate the aspect in the aspectarian. As I am looking for progressions to coincide with September 1968 I start by looking in the aspectarian on 17 April 1957 (= 5 July 1968). There is no Sun conjunct Venus listed. This means that the aspect has already happened or is yet to happen, so look a few days either side. In this case it is separating as the contact was exact on 14 April.

- Note the time that the aspect is exact. In this example the aspectarian list gives Sun trine Venus exactly at 13.39.

- If a day equals a year and 24 hours equals 12 months—as established for the ACD—then any given hour and minutes can also be converted into months and days. So, 13 hours and 39 minutes = 6 months and 3 weeks.

- Add this answer to the corresponding date. In this case 0h 14 April 1957 corresponds to 5 July 1965. Adding 6 months and 3 weeks brings you to the end of January 1966. This is the date when the progressed Sun is exactly conjunct progressed Venus in Emma's chart.

Is it relevant? No. Not only is this a separating aspect, but it was exact more than two and a half years before the date in question. It is therefore history and irrelevant for now.

VENUS PROGRESSED TRINE PLUTO

Follow exactly the same technique as demonstrated for Mars progressed to conjunct Moon.

- When is the applying planet at the same degree and minute as the natal planet?
  When is progressed Venus at 28.11 Aries? Locate the two dates in the ephemerides that encompass this position: 0h 17 April 1957 (= 5 July 1968)—Venus is at 27.21 Aries.

0h 18 April 1957 (= 5 July 1969)—Venus has reached 28.35 Aries.

- **What is the daily motion?**
  In this example Venus has moved from 27♈21 to 28♈35, so the daily motion is 74 minutes of arc.

- **What is the arc?**
  The distance between Venus at its 0h position of 27♈21 to natal Pluto at 28♌11 is 50 minutes of arc.

- **The formula**
  Divide the arc by the daily motion and then multiply by 12: 50 divided by 74, multiplied by 12 = 8.11. The answer is 8 months and 0.11 of a month.

- **The answer**
  Add your answer to the first 0h date of 5 July 1968, so the final answer is 8 March 1969. This is when progressed Venus is exactly trine natal Pluto.

  Is it relevant? Yes. This progression is applying and shows how progressions can come to life six months before being exact. It also shows progressed Venus picking up natal and progressed Pluto.

VENUS PROGRESSED TRINE PROGRESSED PLUTO

Follow exactly the same technique as demonstrated for the progressed Sun conjunct progressed Venus.

- Locate the aspect in the aspectarian. On 17 April 1957 (= 5 July 1968), Venus is trine Pluto. This is listed as the last aspect for that day.

- Note the time that the aspect is exact. In this example the aspectarian lists Venus trine Pluto at exactly 13.31.

- Convert the hours and minutes into months and weeks. So, 13 hours and 31 minutes = 6 months and 3 weeks.

- Add this answer to the corresponding date. In this case 0h 17 April 1957 corresponds to 5 July 1968. Adding 6 months and 3 weeks brings you forward to 26 January 1969. This is the date when progressed Venus is exactly trine progressed Pluto in Emma's chart.

  Is it relevant? Yes. This is an applying progression, involving the chart ruler Venus. It also perfects in the same month as the Neptune-Mercury opposition, showing this time in her life to be highly sensitized.

  Of the six possible progressions, further investigation establishes that only four are relevant in terms of timing. All four are major progressions, involving slow-moving planets and Venus, the chart ruler. These can now be interpreted within the context of Emma's story.

EMMA'S STORY

The event in Emma's life in September 1968 that she remembers so vividly is when she was sent to boarding school at the tender age of 11. As for many children, this proved to be a traumatic experience. Not only did she dislike the school intensely but it also signaled the end of her closeness with her family, her parents and three siblings. From this time onward she found it impossible to talk about personal matters with her parents. In her own words, "Since then we have only ever talked about things, not feelings." Note how this statement is reflected natally in the Moon (feelings) opposite Saturn (denial) and how the missing element of water among the personal planets testifies to the lack of empathy toward her individual needs.

In terms of the progressions this event is powerfully reflected in the Mars-Moon contact, a particularly painful planetary combination. Mars, the knife, cuts the cord that binds her to her mother and her childhood, the Moon. Natally, with a Cancer-Capricorn MC/IC axis, her parents are signified by the rulers of these two signs, the Moon and Saturn. Her mother is clearly the Moon in Gemini in the ninth house, being German and bilingual, and her father is represented by Saturn. The Moon/Saturn opposition also speaks of Emma's disappointment with her mother for not teaching her German. Emma still regrets not acquiring a second language in her childhood and feels this was a missed opportunity.

The Venus-Pluto contacts are also highly descriptive. With a Libra Ascendant, Venus is her ruling planet, in detriment in Aries in the seventh house, putting a strong focus on relating—her personal needs versus the demands and skills of partnership, an issue that became stronger as she grew older. Venus is also combust—burned up by being less than seven and a half degrees away from the Sun. Venus in Aries so often speaks of loneliness or vulnerability, and this was certainly the case when Venus progressed to Pluto—she felt as if she had disappeared. During her first months at boarding school she had no choice but to endure the death of her old, secure life.

As for the Neptune-Mercury progression it is, fittingly, still shrouded in mystery. This is an extremely rare progression and an astrologer would expect it to speak of more than confusion or loneliness, which, although sad, are not uncommon in the transition from childhood to adolescence, especially when sent away from home. With natal Mercury on the eighth cusp—the house of fears, dread, death, and sex—it may well be that this early trauma put her severely at risk, if not physically then emotionally.

Look at how the transits flesh out the progressions. In October came her first Jupiter return—the start of secondary education—but this is a sad Jupiter, in detriment in Virgo, retrograde, square to the Moon, and hiding out in the 12th house. Note how this planet bears witness to missed (12th house) opportunities (Jupiter) through the foreign bilingual mother (Moon in Gemini in the ninth house). Also, Pluto was poised to start his three-legged transit over Jupiter, with the first contact coming in November. So often a planet that is featured in progressions (e.g. Emma's Venus-Pluto) is picked up again in current transits (Pluto transiting Jupiter.)

To complete the picture there was a total eclipse of the Sun on 22 September at 29.30 Virgo, close to the troubled Jupiter at 24.31 Virgo. Even more potent was a total eclipse of the Moon at 13.17 Aries on 6 October—almost exactly conjunct her ruling planet, Venus at 13.25 Aries. When Emma said that she was miserable and lonely, that her family life stopped, and that she felt completely abandoned, it is not difficult to believe her.

PROGRESSING THE ANGLES

If you look back at the diagram for Emma's life for 5 July 1968 (see page 117) you will see that there is one major progression that I have not yet covered. This was the progressed Ascendant at 15.41 Libra opposite her natal Sun in Aries and it was exact at the beginning of October 1968.

The position of the progressed Ascendant in Emma's chart appeared to reinforce the main issue of having independence thrust upon her when she wasn't ready or prepared for it. As an Aries she fought against it, but to no avail. In Emma's example we have a complete and vivid picture without adding this progression, but it is nevertheless a powerful addition.

More importantly, the progressed Ascendant picking out the Sun at this time testifies to the radicality of the chart. The angles of any horoscope, being ascertained only through the time of birth, are extremely sensitive when it comes to timing measures and often act as a guide to the accuracy of the birth time. In natal calculations the Midheaven moves on approximately one degree every five minutes, so a 15-minute discrepancy in the birth time can make a difference of three degrees on this angle, which would then in turn make a difference to the degree on the Ascendant. In natal terms such differences do not usually dramatically change a chart, but it is different with progressions. By progression the Midheaven moves on one degree a year, so a discrepancy of 15 minutes in the birth time then translates into being three years adrift on timings.

Emma's given birth time of 18.00 GMT is probably an approximation but even if you don't have a birth time recorded to the exact minute it is always worth progressing the angles to see what shows. In this example the progressed Ascendant opposing the Sun fits the events, rendering it symbolically appropriate, and other progressions involving the angles for other events in Emma's life also showed the angles of the chart to be reliable.

HOW TO CALCULATE THE PROGRESSED ANGLES

There is more than one way of progressing the angles but the easiest method, and the one I use myself, is called SAL—Solar Arc in Longitude. The basic principle is that the Midheaven moves on at exactly the same rate as the Sun.

- For any year find the progressed Sun. In Emma's chart at 0h on 17 April 1957 (= 5 July 1968) the progressed Sun is at 26.43 Aries.

- Find the difference between the natal and progressed Sun—how far has the Sun moved on from its natal position? The natal Sun is 15.41 Aries so it has moved on 11 degrees and 02 minutes.

- Add this figure to the natal Midheaven. I rounded up Emma's Midheaven to 10 Cancer, but her exact Midheaven is 9.54 Cancer. I now add 11.02, which gives 20.56 Cancer. This is Emma's progressed Midheaven for her year beginning 5 July 1968.

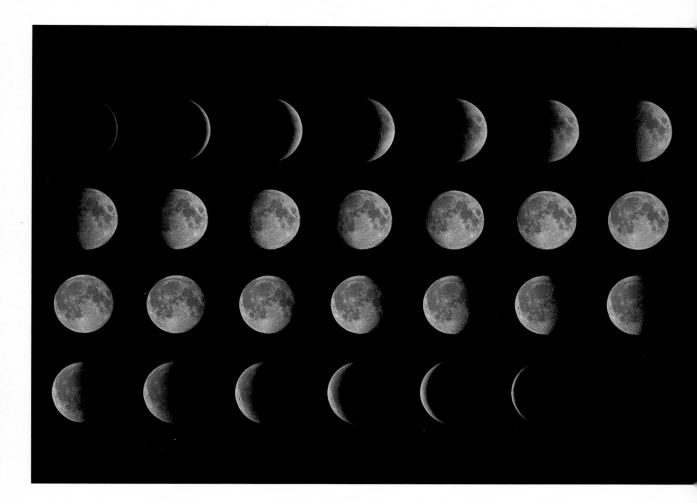

Progressed Ascendant—no calculations are necessary. Simply look up the progressed Midheaven (10th cusp) in the Tables of Houses (using the same latitude as for natal calculations) and read off the corresponding Ascendant. Emma's place of birth is at 53N19, with the nearest tables being at 53N25. A Midheaven of nearly 21 Cancer gives an Ascendant of approximately 15.30 Libra. Accuracy to within a quarter of a degree is all that is necessary.

THE PROGRESSED MOON

In progressions the Moon needs to be treated separately because it moves so swiftly. The Moon travels through all 12 signs once every 28 days, so in terms of progressions the Moon travels through all 12 signs once every 28 years. This makes the Moon a unique factor because it is not possible for any other planet to make the full orbit by progression.

As a rough guide the Moon progresses by one degree a month, but there is an

The Moon moves swiftly through the 12 signs once every 28 days. Regarding progressions, it travels through the 12 signs once every 28 years.

easy way to assure greater accuracy. This is to divide the Moon's daily motion by 12 (months in a year) so that you can see exactly where it is month by month. For example, we can track the progressed Moon in Emma's chart from July 1993 to July 1994:

- 0h 12 May 1957 (= 5 July 1993)—the Moon is at 26.01 Libra

  0h 13 May 1957 (= 5 July 1994)—the Moon has reached 9.58 Scorpio

- The Moon's daily motion—the distance it moves in this 24-hour period—is 13 degrees and 57 minutes. Convert the daily motion into the total number of minutes: 13 x 60 + 57 = 837.

- Divide the answer by 12. 837 divided by 12 = 69.7, which we round up to 1 degree and 10 minutes.

- Now move the Moon on by 1 degree and 10 minutes for each month, noting the aspects it makes as it travels around the chart. Use the initial "p" after a planet to refer to its progressed position.

For this example year beginning July 1993, see the box opposite. By the end of the calculations in the box, I am three minutes of arc adrift, but this is such a negligible amount that you can simply "lose" it at the end of your list.

THE PROGRESSED MOON IN INTERPRETATION

I was many years into my astrological studies before I fully realized the importance of the progressed Moon. In many ways the progressed Moon can act as a testimony to the bigger picture, in the same way as we have seen with lunations and eclipses. Because it moves so quickly, the time when the progressed Moon is making an exact aspect, especially by conjunction, is a highly sensitized time. In terms of prediction the progressed Moon can act as a marker, narrowing down the time scale for a coming event. Note that in the example for Emma, the progressed Moon was in aspect to her progressed Mars—ruler of the seventh—in February, the month that she left her husband.

Date	Position
5 JULY 1993 *sextile Pluto p*	26.01 LIBRA
5 AUGUST 1993 *sextile Pluto and quinqunx Venus*	27.11 LIBRA
5 SEPTEMBER 1993	28.21 LIBRA
5 OCTOBER 1993	29.31 LIBRA
5 NOVEMBER 1993 *conjunct Neptune p*	00.41 SCORPIO
5 DECEMBER 1993 *conjunct Neptune, opposite Mercury, square Uranus*	01.51 SCORPIO
5 JANUARY 1994 *square Uranus p*	03.01 SCORPIO
5 FEBRUARY 1994 *trine Mars p*	04.11 SCORPIO
5 MARCH 1994	05.21 SCORPIO
5 APRIL 1994	06.31 SCORPIO
5 MAY 1994	07.41 SCORPIO
5 JUNE 1994	08.51 SCORPIO
5 JULY 1994 *trine Midheaven*	09.58 (10.01) SCORPIO

WILL I EVER HAVE A BABY?

As already discussed with regard to lunations, the Moon, with its connection to women and fertility, is enormously important when it comes to questions about children. Some years ago I did a Tarot reading in January for a young woman in which I predicted a baby, a pronouncement that unleashed both excitement and disbelief. I was pretty confident about the reading but I was less sure of the timing. Among other positive cards the reading included the Empress in the near future, a beautiful card for fertility and motherhood, so I said that she would fall pregnant very soon. When she pushed me to be more precise I plumped for April.

This wasn't good enough. She wanted an exact date, so I suggested that we look at her horoscope as I felt that I would then be on surer ground with regard to timing, and she agreed. It turned out that the main reason for her disbelief, apart from natural cynicism, was that she and her husband had been trying for a baby for a couple of years without success. She was now beginning to wonder if she would ever have a child, and for a woman who is desperate to have a family there is no worse anxiety.

EARTHY TAURUS

The first corroborating evidence in the horoscope of the Empress card in the Tarot reading was as good as I could hope for—she had Venus in dignity in earthy Taurus conjunct the fifth cusp—the house of children. What better symbol of "the earth mother" could an astrologer ask for? However, it was in a wide opposition—nearly at the full eight-degree orb—to the Moon in Scorpio, her sign of fall. This placing often indicates gynecological problems, which she confirmed as the source of her anxiety. With an opposition always look for an outlet—and here was the perfect one. The Moon disposited Jupiter in his sign of exaltation, Cancer, in the seventh house, and

Jupiter was trine the Moon and sextile Venus. I had no doubt that she would conceive, but she still wanted an exact date and nothing else would do.

With fingers crossed I looked at the timings. The main progression was the progressed Ascendant—which, representing the physical body can be another important indicator for pregnancy—opposing Jupiter, the outlet for the Moon/Venus opposition. This progression was exact in the second week of April, tying in with the timing from the Tarot reading. As testimony to this picture the progressed Moon was approaching the Ascendant, and would be exactly conjunct the Ascendant at the very beginning of April. I therefore predicted that she could conceive around the beginning of the month and I had to assure her that I couldn't be any more precise. She phoned me a couple of months after the reading, overjoyed, with the news that she had in fact conceived in the middle of March. This was when the progressed Ascendant

was still applying to the opposition of Jupiter, and the progressed Moon applying to conjunct the Ascendant, being half a degree away at the time of conception.

This story confirms the potency of applying progressions. You may like to note that there were no major transits in operation at the time, which confirms that working with transits alone is insufficient.

WILL I MEET A NEW MAN SOON?

Using the progressed Moon as a marker was a very helpful device in this reading. A woman in her forties, divorced for two years, had recovered enough to start thinking about another relationship. There were no major progressions in evidence but she was in the middle of a three-legged Jupiter transit over Mars, who

was ruler of her seventh house of partnership and positioned in the 11th house—friends and organizations. If nothing else this seemed to bode well for a burgeoning social life, which could only stack the odds in her favor when it came to romantic opportunities. Being an outgoing Sagittarian she had no trouble with mixing and mingling, and she confirmed that her social life could hardly be better—in fact, it was a struggle to get a night in.

The most encouraging feature of her chart was to be found in the progressed Moon, which was applying to within one degree of her Descendant—the angle to the seventh house. As a long shot I asked her whom she had met 28 years ago—the last time that the Moon would have been conjunct her Descendant. She had to

think for a while but then it came to her. She had met her first serious boyfriend when she was 16 and they had got engaged the following year, the time when the Moon was conjunct her Descendant. The engagement had been broken off after she had moved away to go to college—they had simply outgrown each other—but she nevertheless had fond memories of this man. From the point of view of the reading this story gave us both faith in the prediction that another relationship was on its way, which it was.

As I recommended when learning transits, there is no better starting point than your own chart and it is a highly educational exercise to progress your own chart for key dates and see what shows. To summarize the points of importance and priority you are looking for:

- Progressed Sun—The Sun progresses at approximately one degree a year. Solar progressions throw light and bring things to life.
- Progressed angles—The axes of the chart are highly sensitive. The progressed angles, or progressions to the angles, generally indicate life-changing events.
- The chart ruler—Progressions involving the chart ruler usually signal major events for the native.
- The progressed Moon—The Moon makes a full orbit every 28 years. Use the progressed Moon as a marker and as a testimony to interpretation. Note especially the aspects made by conjunction, and when it changes sign, which will be approximately every two and a half years.
- Critical degrees—When the Moon or any other planet progresses to 29 degrees (the end of a sign) or to 0 degrees (the beginning of the next sign) these are said to be critical degrees, that is, important in terms of opening up a new chapter.
- Universal versus particular—Consider any planet involved in a progression in terms of both its universal and particular symbolism.
- Stations—If a planet is retrograde at birth, check to see when it goes direct by progression. Conversely,

does any planet turn retrograde by progression? These dates are likely to yield literal "turning points" in the native's life.

- Aspects—You will find that the major aspects are usually the most potent when locating and interpreting progressions. However, minor aspects can also tell a story and are worth investigating, especially if they involve slow-moving planets, the angles, the Sun, or the chart ruler. The quinqunx, for example, can often indicate illness or accidents by progression.
- Transits—See how the transits flesh out the picture being painted by the progressions. Note especially if a transiting planet is also being picked out in a progression, and therefore underlining a theme.

With a sound grasp of progressions as an exercise from mathematics to meaning you can bring any horoscope to life for any given date. What if there are no major progressions for a particular date? Simple— there aren't any. Look for when the next major progressions come into play and stick with the current transits, even of the personal planets. The moment you start hunting for things to plug the gap your interpretations are likely to misfire. But have faith in the fact that it is unusual for nothing to show when someone has bothered to seek out an astrologer. Usually your problem will be the reverse—cutting through the activity to isolate what is important and relevant to the client's story. In many ways, working with progressions brings the astrologer full circle, as, in either natal or progressed work, the degree of accuracy and success lies always in your understanding and connection with astrological symbolism.

The horoscope speaks not just of the individual but also of other people in that person's life and, for a practicing astrologer, questions about love and relationships are by far the most common. This chapter illustrates how to identify the natal promise and timings—the kind of relationships someone is likely to have and when they are likely to have them. Learning to interpret "synastry," astrological compatibility as revealed by the comparison of two horoscopes, is also a fascinating and valuable tool in this area of astrology.

RELATIONSHIPS

RELATIONSHIPS

There are no prizes for guessing the issues about which I am most commonly asked. A practicing astrologer is asked about love, romance, and marriage time and time again. At a rough estimate I would say that, in my own practice, seven out of ten consultations are about relationships. This makes for a mixed bag of readings as you find yourself dealing with everything from the excitement of new attractions to the pain of love gone wrong and bitter endings.

WHAT TO LOOK FOR

The astrologer's first task is to assess what is called the natal promise. In other words, what kind of relationships is someone likely to experience in his or her life? Every chart needs to be assessed in its own right but these guidelines will point you in the right direction:

The seventh house The seventh cusp is the Descendant, the angle that marks the beginning of the house of partnership and of all important, one-to-one relationships. Lovers are often assigned to the fifth house but, in my experience, fifth-house encounters are in the category of one-night stands or holiday romances. Any serious relationship matters are always located in the seventh. Look for the ruler of the seventh house—the planet that rules the sign on the cusp. Assess the condition of this planet by sign, house, and aspect, as this planet will describe the partner.

The first house Locate the chart ruler, as this planet is the particular significator for the native and note especially if it is in aspect to the ruler of the seventh house. If the two planets are in a positive aspect, this bodes well for successful relationships. If the two planets are in a difficult aspect, this indicates that the love life of the native will be more of a struggle. If the two planets are not in any aspect at all, this does not mean that there won't be any relationships, but you will have to be guided by other factors.

Planets in the seventh house Consider the condition of any planets posited in the seventh house, and especially any planets conjunct the seventh cusp—within five degrees either side of the cusp. Any planets in the seventh house will add further information to the type of relationship experiences the native is likely to encounter. For example, the benefics Jupiter or Venus in the seventh house would be considered as big plus points, whereas the malefic planets would be considered not necessarily as unfortunate but more complex.

Venus and Mars These two planets are the universal significators for love and romance, women and men.

The lights Note the condition of the Moon as it is very much linked to our emotional needs. The Moon in the seventh or the first house tends to put extra emphasis on the importance or need for partnership, especially in a man's chart. Similarly, the Sun in the seventh or the first house is especially strong for a woman. As with Venus and Mars, a positive aspect between the Sun (men/masculine) and the Moon (women/feminine) also bodes very well for romance.

SYNASTRY

Synastry means compatibility, as revealed by the comparison of two horoscopes. This is a fascinating area of astrological study as it shows both the strengths of a relationship and also the areas of difference or conflict. Through a careful examination of both the negative and positive contacts, showing how the two charts interact with each other, astrology can go a long way toward assessing and understanding the nature of a relationship, such as attraction, why we may hit it off instantly with one person but dislike another on sight, the chances of a relationship lasting, those who are good or bad for us, and so on.

If you are dealing with a question about a relationship it is always a good idea to ask for the partner's data. If you don't have the partner's chart, you can still check in the ephemerides for the signs of the planets, but you won't have the all-important horizon of the Ascendant and Descendant signs, or the exact position of the Moon, which are vital points of reference in synastry. The closest you can get is to calculate a "noon chart," finding the position of the planets at midday to give you an approximated picture, and this can still be very informative.

There is an easy way to do "at a glance" synastry and this is by using the method that I demonstrated in chapter six for progressions. Using squared paper write the degrees 0–30 along the top. Then write the planet and the planet's sign underneath the corresponding degree number, one row for each person. You will then see immediately which planets or angles in one chart line up with planets or angles in the other, e.g., between Catherine Zeta-Jones and Michael Douglas.

You will find Catherine Zeta-Jones' chart on page 61 in chapter four. Michael Douglas' exact planets and angles are:

Ascendant	27.03	*Scorpio*
Midheaven	10.54	*Virgo*
Sun	2.26	*Libra*
Moon	4.09	*Capricorn*
Mercury	15.02	*Virgo*
Venus	26.48	*Libra*
Mars	18.03	*Libra*
Jupiter	13.11	*Virgo*
Saturn	10.06	*Cancer*
Uranus	13.07	*Gemini*
Neptune	3.56	*Libra*
Pluto	9.48	*Leo*
North Node	25.04	*Cancer*
Part of Fortune	28.46	*Aquarius*

In synastry the major aspects are the most important—conjunction, opposition, square, trine, or sextile. Astrologers differ on the orbs allowed for synastry contacts, some being more generous than others. I usually allow up to a three-degree orb in chart comparison but, as with locating aspects in the natal chart or by progression, the tighter the orb the more powerful the contact. By comparing Catherine Zeta-Jones' planets and angles with those of her husband we can locate the synastry between them. The synastry contacts start with her Sun conjunct his Sun as they share the same birthday of September 25.

CATHERINE ZETA-JONES	ASPECT	MICHAEL DOUGLAS
Sun and Uranus	Conjunct Square	Sun and Neptune Moon
Mars	Conjunct Square	Sun and Neptune Moon
Venus	Trine	Moon
Mercury, ruler of seventh house	Square Sextile	Saturn Pluto
Jupiter, chart ruler	Trine	Uranus
Part of Fortune	Trine	Mars—chart ruler
Pluto	Sextile	North Node
Midheaven	Conjunct	Venus—ruler of seventh house
Neptune	Conjunct	Ascendant
Moon	Trine	Ascendant

This synastry exercise reveals a high number of positive contacts between the two charts and this couple therefore scores high on the compatibility scale. The most difficult contact, and the one I would explore in a consultation, is her Mercury square his Saturn. This is important because Mercury is the ruler of her seventh house, and is therefore the prime significator for her partner, and it is in a stressful aspect to his Saturn in Cancer, in detriment. We can only speculate what this might mean for them in the particular, but at a universal level the astrologer could start by exploring how he might repress or control (Saturn) her expression (Mercury), or how the age

gap (Saturn ruling age) might hinder communication (Mercury) on certain matters. Exploring universal symbolism will nearly always lead the consultation toward uncovering the particular.

MORE THAN JUST SUN SIGNS

Many people think that the Sun sign is vital in compatibility and I am always being asked which sign is "good for" another. In fact compatibility between the Moon signs is more important as the Moon relates to our emotional nature. In popular astrology you will learn that being "in your element" is a basic guideline, that fire signs get on with the other fire signs, water with water, and so on. While this may be true at one level, the art of synastry goes deeper than this, showing that those who are supposedly incompatible by Sun sign can actually have a strong relationship that is symbolized by other astrological factors.

A couple who recently celebrated their silver wedding anniversary are a prime example of this. By Sun sign she is an Aries and he is a Cancer, and both are typical of their sign. Unsurprisingly, then, she is in many ways the driving force behind the relationship. She is always on the go, always getting things done quickly and efficiently, always thinking about the next project, and thrives on achievement. He is home-loving, kind and careful with other people, cautious by nature, and likes to do things in his own time. There are times when the Aries woman may call her Cancer man slow. Conversely, there are times when he may think she is bossy or spending too much money. With Aries and Cancer being square to each other, a stressful aspect, such different approaches to life show the astrological conflict of the Sun signs as essential natures in the external world. But the longevity and closeness of this successful marriage is clearly located in other synastry, the key factor of which is her Venus exalted in Pisces, conjunct his Descendant in Pisces—the angle of the seventh house of partnership.

Powerful contacts such as this will override relatively minor differences such as incompatible Sun signs.

THE COSMIC MARRIAGE

When you are locating synastry one of the most powerful symbols of union is "a cosmic marriage"—when one person's Sun is in the same sign and within five degrees of the other person's Moon. For example,

◆ Jennifer Aniston has the Moon at 23.15 Sagittarius. I don't know the time of birth of her husband Brad Pitt, but he was born on 18 December 1963 in Shawnee, Oklahoma. The Sun at midday is at 26.06 Sagittarius and as the Sun moves on at a rate of one degree a day, this is a correct position to within half a degree. This gives them a cosmic marriage of her Moon and his Sun in the same sign and within five degrees of each other.

A cosmic marriage doesn't apply just to love and marriage but can feature in any close relationship.

◆ A famous example of an almost exact cosmic marriage is the Queen's Sun at 0.13 Taurus and Prince Charles' Moon at 0.26 Taurus.

◆ Sarah Ferguson has a cosmic marriage with her second daughter. Sarah's Moon is at 6.37 Aries, conjunct Princess Eugenie's Sun at 2.56 Aries.

I am fortunate enough to have experienced cosmic marriages twice in my life, once with my mother—my Moon in the same sign and at exactly the same degree as her Sun—and with my husband. My Sun is at 9 degrees of Sagittarius and his Moon is at 8 degrees of the same sign. This certainly doesn't mean that we never have problems, but the cosmic marriage speaks of a powerful bond, a sense of belonging, no matter what your other differences might be.

If one person's Sun sign is the same as the other person's Moon sign, but not within five degrees of each other, this is not strictly a cosmic marriage. Nevertheless, it still symbolizes a very strong bond and sense of identity with the other. For example:

◆ Sir Paul McCartney's Sun is at 26 degrees of Gemini. I don't know the time of birth of his wife Heather Mills, but on her date of birth, 12 January 1968, the Moon travels from 8 to nearly 21 degrees of Gemini. We do not know the exact degree of her Moon, but we know that it is definitely in this sign.

The same applies to the doubling up of signs with any combination of the Sun, Moon, Ascendant, and Descendant, showing how the charts reflect each other. For example:

◆ John Lennon's Sun was at 16.16 Libra and his Moon was at 3.32 Aquarius. He married Yoko Ono, who has an Ascendant at 8.30 Libra and the Sun at 29.23 Aquarius.

OTHER POWERFUL SYNASTRY

Apart from the cosmic marriage there are other powerful contacts to look out for. In particular, if either of the Lights—the Sun or the Moon—is conjunct the other person's Ascendant or Descendant to within five degrees, this can speak of strong attraction and every possibility of a lasting union. Just as powerful can be one person's Venus conjunct the other person's Ascendant or Descendant, especially if Venus is in a good sign, as in the example of the Aries woman and Cancer man quoted above. Harmonious contacts with generous Jupiter, the other benefic, can also be considered as highly fortunate. Contacts with Mercury are also worth noting as the closeness and success of a relationship so often comes down to the ability to communicate. For example:

◆ The closest synastry contact between Edward VIII and Wallis Simpson, the woman for whom he gave up the throne, is Edward's Mercury at 27.37 of Cancer, almost exactly conjunct Wallis Simpson's Ascendant of 27.30 Cancer.

Another powerful contact is when both of the chart rulers or the rulers of the seventh house are conjunct. Also look out for charts that have the same Ascendant.

If the rising degree is the same to within five degrees, then the two people will share the same horizon, looking out at the world through a shared lens.

SATURN AND THE OUTER PLANETS

If Saturn or any of the outer planets—Uranus, Neptune, and Pluto—are posited in the seventh house, then the arena of relationships is likely to be more complicated, but the astrologer must always keep an open mind. It is too easy to think of Saturn, for example, as a negating factor. But just as Saturn in the second house does not mean "no money" (Prince Charles has Saturn in the second house) Saturn in the seventh house does not deny love, as illustrated with Jennifer Aniston's chart later in this chapter.

I personally feel that others come into our lives when they are meant to, we learn what we need to from them and they from us, and the so-called malefic planets in the seventh house or in synastry can symbolize steep learning curves but still be powerful in terms of attraction and attachment. As always, each case needs to be judged in its own right and in its own context. As with all astrology, start by looking for universal symbolism.

SERIOUS LOVE
Saturn in the seventh house

In the pursuit of romantic love we may be resistant to the idea of "working at" relationships but, as Saturn is exalted in the seventh-house sign of Libra, astrology tells us that love is inextricably bound up with effort, discipline, and emotional maturity. Saturn signals boundaries that have to be collapsed and then reinstated in the process of falling in love and then staying in love. The individual with Saturn in the seventh may need to learn how to share, compromise, and incorporate another into his

or her life. Or this person may exercise extreme caution when it comes to letting others get close. Conversely, he or she may attract Saturnian types. With Saturn in the seventh, or as ruler of the seventh, it is not uncommon to attract older partners. I have also found that the same often applies when any planet ruling the seventh is in Saturn's feminine sign of Capricorn. A client of mine has Jupiter in Capricorn as ruler of the seventh and is happily married to a woman ten years his senior. The time of the Saturn return is especially important if Saturn is in or ruler of the seventh.

SATURN IN SYNASTRY

Saturn contacts may be experienced as denial in some form, such as being with someone who can't give you what you really want or who keeps you at arm's length. Or it can put the brakes on the development of a relationship, or symbolize the brick wall, not being able to get through to someone. The flip side of the coin is that positive Saturn inter-aspects can also be experienced as steadying and stabilizing, providing firm foundations for enduring love. Some astrologers take the line that Saturn contacts point to karmic relationships, which is another fascinating area of study.

"When Yoko came into my life nothing else seemed important. Her work and her way of life just blew my mind open."

John Lennon

WILD LOVE
Uranus in the seventh house

The individual with Uranus in the seventh is likely to have a volatile love life. This placing can point to relationships that start and stop dramatically, unexpectedly, or explosively. Or they may be unconventional in some way. The time of the Uranus half-return is especially important if Uranus is in the seventh, or if Aquarius is on the Descendant, picking out Uranus as the co-ruler of the seventh house.

URANUS IN SYNASTRY

It is not within the scope of this book to compare each planet but the nature of synastry contacts will vary depending on the particular planets involved. This is especially important with Uranus, as it is a bit of a loose cannon. Positive Uranus-Venus contacts, for example, can be exciting and highly stimulating, but difficult Uranus-Mars contacts could flag up an angry or even violent combination.

Yoko Ono has the Sun, Venus, and Saturn all in Aquarius in the fifth and she also has a seventh-house Uranus, so an astrologer would expect Uranian symbolism to show in her love life. She met John Lennon in 1968 and their shared astrological themes have already been mentioned. But their key synastry that supports the bigger picture lies in the powerful combination of her seventh-house Uranus at 20.33 Aries being conjunct Lennon's Ascendant at 19.41 Aries—so less than one degree apart.

ROMANTIC OR REDEEMING LOVE
Neptune in the seventh

As already stated in chapter five, relationships that come together under Neptune can be the heady stuff of fairy tales, but they then have to stand the test of reality if they are going to last. An individual with Neptune in the seventh house faces this challenge as there may be a tendency to over-romanticize or to fall prey to self-deception. Seeking the idealized union, the perfect soul mate, can too easily lead to unrealistic expectations of a partner. Neptune is connected with sacrifice or martyrdom, so there may also be a tendency to "rescue," entering into a relationship with someone who is needy and who then can quickly become dependent.

NEPTUNE IN SYNASTRY

The same themes can feature in Neptune synastry. Inter-aspects with this planet can point to relationships

that are highly romantic, even to the extent of being mesmerized with someone. There may be a risk of idealizing the person with whom you have Neptune synastry, which in turn increases the risk of disillusionment. On a more positive note, Neptune synastry can also signal a deep spiritual connection with another as well as "glamorous" love. Note the two-way Neptune synastry for Michael Douglas and Catherine Zeta-Jones:

Her Neptune at 26.34 Scorpio conjunct his Ascendant at 27.03 Scorpio.

His Neptune at 3.56 Libra conjunct her Sun at 2.19 Libra, Uranus at 4.16 Libra.

OBSESSIVE OR HEALING LOVE
Pluto in the seventh

Plutonic symbolism related to the seventh house can point to obsessions or control issues, or deep, powerful attractions. Unless there is a high level of self-awareness and commitment on both sides, there is a higher risk of jealousy, possessiveness, overpowering intensity, or game playing. The uncompromising, all-or-nothing nature of Pluto generally indicates intense relationships that bring profound emotional experiences, for good or ill—destructive at worst, therapeutic and healing at best. Freud, the founder of psychoanalysis, has Pluto conjunct the Descendant.

A lady in her fifties with Pluto in the seventh confirmed that her whole life had been dominated and continually changed by powerful relationships. The Pluto symbolism of absence and endings was shown by the death of her first husband at a young age, and a divorce from her second husband. At the time of the consultation she was married for the third time to a man who embodied positive, transformative Pluto qualities, being a spiritualist and also a healer.

CASE STUDY   JENNIFER DOMINATED BY SATURN

Jennifer Aniston's horoscope is a clear example of effective astrological symbolism.

Natal promise With a Libra Ascendant, Jennifer Aniston has Aries on the Descendant. The significator for her partner is therefore Mars. Mars is dignified in Scorpio, placed tightly on the second-house cusp and conjunct Neptune in Scorpio, wonderful symbolism for millionaire movie star Brad Pitt. A dignified Mars (strong masculine type) in sexy Scorpio, conjunct Neptune (charisma, film), on the second-house cusp (money).

Chart ruler Venus at nine degrees of Aries is in detriment and not in aspect to Mars. However, she has synastry here with Brad Pitt as his

Jupiter is also at nine degrees Aries. The two benefics in conjunction is extremely positive.

The lights The Sun and Moon are in harmony, in an almost exact sextile. As already pointed out, her Moon is also conjunct his Sun, giving them the cosmic marriage.

The seventh house Saturn is conjunct the Descendant, in Aries, its sign of fall, but this is eased by the Sun and Saturn being in a mixed reception—the Sun is in Saturn's sign of Aquarius and Saturn is in the Sun's sign of exaltation, Aries. If you make the reception—change the sign but hold the degree—the Sun "moves" to 23.22 Aries, conjunct the Descendant and illuminating the marriage angle. Saturn is also trine the Moon and this trine is

mediated by the Sun, who is in sextile to both.

Timing measures These confirm the important positive pattern of the Moon, Sun, and Saturn.

Meeting Jennifer Aniston met Brad Pitt in spring 1998, at the time of her Saturn return, which was exact on 26 March 1998. This confirms the dominance of the angular, well-aspected Saturn in her love life. Brad Pitt's chart also has a strong Saturnian theme—he has a dignified Saturn in Aquarius, dispositing four planets in Saturn's other sign of Capricorn, including both the feminine planets of the Moon and Venus, along with Mercury and Mars. The two charts therefore complement each other.

Marriage Jennifer Aniston and Brad Pitt married on 29 July 2000.

PLUTO IN SYNASTRY

Relationships that feature Pluto inter-aspects can signal the same themes as Pluto in the seventh house. With self-awareness such contacts can offer the possibility of mutually empowering relationships. The worst-case scenario is that Pluto contacts show relationships that operate through the abuse of power. I remember an example of a young woman who felt dominated and intimidated by her boss. The synastry showed that her Moon was conjunct her boss' Pluto.

TIMING MEASURES FOR RELATIONSHIPS

When locating progressions for relationships look for the same planets as when locating relationships in the natal chart:

Progressed rulers of the seventh and the first house
If these two planets come together by progression—making any aspect between them—this is a traditional indication of an important relationship.

Progressed Sun Solar progressions are always powerful. Look for the Sun progressed to the ruler of the seventh or to planets in the seventh. Also look for

- ◆ The natal promise of the positive aspect between the Sun and Moon is delivered as the lights come together at the time of the marriage. Her progressed Moon was at 23.12 Aquarius, applying by just 20 minutes of arc to a conjunction of the Sun.
- ◆ Progressed Saturn was at 24.23 Aries, applying by 7 minutes of arc to a conjunction with the marriage angle, the Descendant, of 24.29 Aries. (With 7 minutes of arc to go, this aspect is not exact until the following year, so it is a fitting progression for the marriage and the first year of marriage.)
- ◆ Her Midheaven was progressed to 28.43 Leo, conjunct Regulus, the benefic fixed star at 29 Leo, denoting fame and fortune.

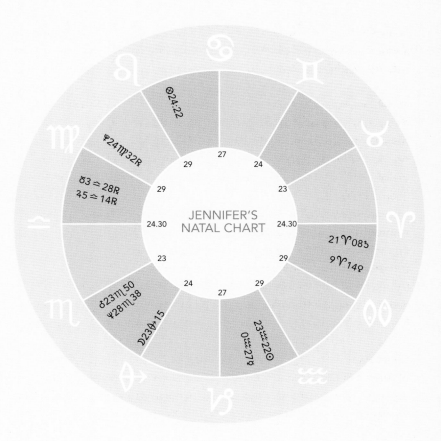

JENNIFER'S NATAL CHART

the Sun progressed to Mars (natal or progressed), or vice versa, Mars to the Sun, in a woman's chart. Look for the Sun progressed to the Moon or Venus, or Venus to the Sun or Moon, in a man's chart.

Venus and Mars If these two planets, the universal significators for love and romance, are coming together by progression, this is also a positive indication for a relationship.

Progressed Moon This is a very helpful indicator when locating specific events. For relationships, look to see if the progressed Moon is conjunct either the first- or seventh-house ruler, any planet in the seventh, the Ascendant or Descendant, or already traveling through the first or seventh house. Other classic indications for romance is when the progressed Moon is conjunct the Sun, Venus, or Mars.

Transits Look especially for transits of the last five planets—Jupiter, Saturn, Uranus, Neptune, and Pluto—to the rulers of either the first or seventh houses, or to any planets in the first or seventh, or the Sun, Moon, Venus, or Mars. Major transits can sometimes signal events single-handedly but, as already discussed, they are more likely to provide a backdrop to the progressed chart. As always, the strength of any transits and progressions are dictated by the condition of natal factors.

LOVE ISSUES IN A CONSULTATION

There are many different kinds of relationships, but no matter what trials someone may be battling with friends, family, or workmates, there is nothing to compare with the emotional minefield of an intimate and sexual relationship. It is in a league of its own. Relationship questions can arise in all sorts of ways and contexts, but the practicing astrologer will mostly encounter three categories:

Singles The first is the single person who wants to know when his or her next relationship will happen, or whether there is a chance with the person he or she is interested in now, or will he or she ever love anyone again?

Married The second is someone who is already in a settled or long-term relationship, not necessarily marriage. This person may want to find out more about his or her partner, may be seeking help over a difficult patch, or may want to know if the relationship is going to last.

Extra Marital The third is someone who is either having an affair, thinking of having one, or whose partner is having one. Dealing with love triangles is extremely tricky but it is a very common occurrence. Affairs, the "forbidden fruit" of love, seem to generate the most intense feelings of all. Does he or she really love me? Will he or she leave and come to me, and if so when and how? These are the sorts of questions the astrologer must be prepared to listen to and deal with.

For most people—whatever their age, relationship status, or sexual orientation—relationship issues are right at the top of the list, and this area of astrology needs very careful and delicate handling. As I have already stated, happy and contented people do not generally seek out astrologers, so a lot of the time you will be dealing with the bleaker side of love, when things are going wrong or there are problems that need to be examined.

BEING ALONE

One of the main messages that has come home to me over the years of my work as an astrologer is the very real fear, sometimes terror, that many people feel at the prospect of being alone, either by continuing a single existence or, more commonly, having to revert to one if a relationship is threatening to end. This fear is of course partly bound up with our social conditioning, but there are other factors in play as well. Even if you could get someone to admit that a relationship is making him or her unhappy, that he or she is unfulfilled or incompatible with the other half, or even the worst-case scenario that the relationship is dangerous or abusive, the person will still have a great deal invested in that relationship. This makes it extremely difficult or even impossible for the person to act on the ultimate solution, namely to leave. The shame of "failure," the fear of what others will say, what there is to lose, such as the loss of status, company, and habit-forming familiarity over the years together, all often add up to something much weightier than what there is to gain in the future. For many people autonomy is merely a pseudonym for loneliness. In the light of this it is easier to understand why many people will only leave an unhappy, unfulfilling relationship when they have found somebody else.

In such scenarios the astrologer can help by exploring the nature of someone's relationships as described in his or her chart and in the synastry with the other person involved. And, whatever the issue, timing measures are always crucial to relationship questions—when did the relationship start, what is happening now, what is going to happen next, what are the future prospects? By piecing together the astrological picture in this way, the nature and sequence of developments become clearer as the horoscope and its timing measures provide a continual frame of reference.

Astrology can also offer both hope and validation. If a relationship is coming to an end, astrology can demonstrate that, just because it didn't last doesn't mean that it wasn't meant to be—quite the opposite—or that there will never be anyone else. For someone who is in crisis a consultation is just as much about comfort as it is about gaining information. And for those who are not in crisis, locating the astrology of relationships can be a lot of fun and probably one of the most pleasurable of the astrologer's challenges.

RUTH FRUSTRATED BY MARS

When Ruth first came to see me she gave very little away of her real feelings, as you would expect from someone with a cautious Virgo Ascendant and her ruler Mercury retrograde in self-contained Cancer, disposited by the Moon in matter-of-fact and objective Aquarius.

When Ruth reappeared at a later date, it was in this session that she saw the therapeutic power of astrology come into play. It was also this session that signaled the importance of Mars in Ruth's chart.

Ruth had married at a very young age, had grown-up children, and had been divorced for many years. In October 1989, about a year after her divorce, she met a man called Chris. He fell for her hook, line, and sinker and the progressions in his chart at this time clearly showed that this was the case. Mercury, lord of Chris'

seventh house (Gemini), was progressed to conjunct the dignified fifth house, Venus in Taurus, and progressed Venus was sextiling the Moon. All the factors that you would expect to see for a major relationship are in play—Venus for love, Moon for the emotions and women, and the particular ruler of the seventh house of partnership.

For Ruth the story of the relationship was not so easy. She had progressed Mars squaring the 12th house Pluto almost to the minute of arc. In other words, two

malefic planets had come together by progression—progressed Mars moving into aspect with natal Pluto. And this major progression was duplicated by transit, as Pluto was transiting opposite natal Mars, making its third and final contact in October 1989, underlining the importance of Pluto and its symbolism at this time. This picture clearly spoke of the post-divorce year as well as the new, obsessive man coming into her life, as Pluto can symbolize both absence and intense or obsessive feelings.

FINDING HERSELF

We had discussed Ruth's Aquarian streak that wanted to categorize and objectify rather than let life and feelings flow in and out. The Pisces Descendant showed that which she needed to seek out for herself rather than experience through "the other." And this theme was mirrored in the progressed chart at the time of meeting Chris—her own Mars, natally square Uranus, had progressed to square Pluto in the year she met him, allowing her to dissociate from her Mars. Mars coming together exactly with Pluto, the planet of absence, destruction, or invisibility, mirrored how she could completely cut off from her desire for, or sexual needs from, men, i.e., Mars. Ruth could not really desire Chris and even after many years could not enact the brutality of Mars in Taurus that was needed to cut him off. Her real struggle was to claim back her anger, desire, and earthy passion so that she did not need other people, i.e. men, to act it out for her.

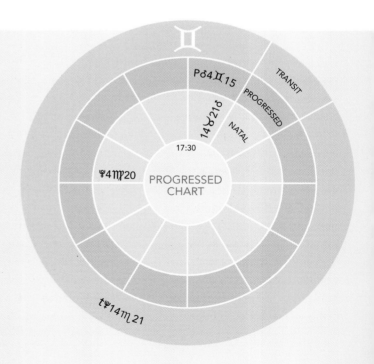

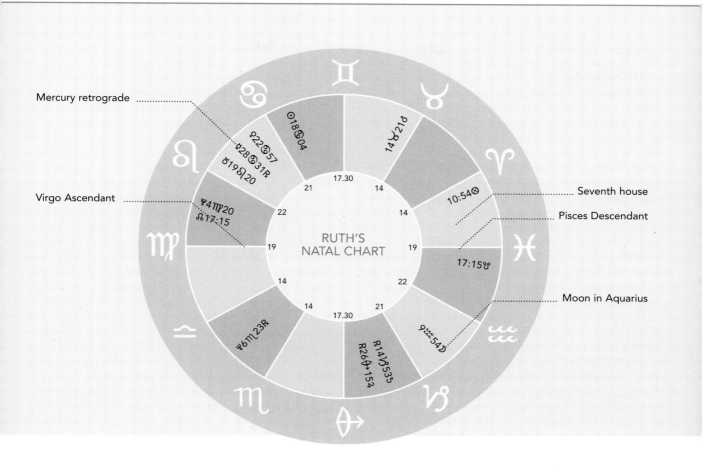

Mercury retrograde

Virgo Ascendant

Seventh house

Pisces Descendant

Moon in Aquarius

RUTH'S NATAL CHART

Neptunian fantasy Ruth was swept along and started the relationship properly in March 1990. It lasted through to November 1991, exactly the duration of a long Neptune transit—co-ruler of her seventh house (Pisces) transiting Saturn. Here is an example of a co-ruler in action as, with Pisces on the Descendant, Neptune had a say over her love life. At a universal level Neptune signifies times of being at sea, either through confusion or the blindness of romantic love, in this case dissolving the personal boundaries that are symbolized by Saturn. Only when Neptune is out of the picture can we distinguish between what is real and what is fantasy.

Even though the relationship ended when she emerged from her Neptunian haze, Chris repeatedly asked her to marry him over the ensuing years and she sometimes wondered if she was making a mistake by refusing. But when I saw the position of his Mars it was clear. At 18:39 Pisces, Mars is the closest point of synastry, conjunct her Descendant by less than half a degree, reflecting his persistence in pressing his suit and his attempts to make her feel sorry for him. Mars in Pisces is a subtle energy but can be very manipulative. The astrology reveals how they had become locked into an emotional battle that neither could win.

When the astrologer goes to work then astrological symbolism comes out to play, as the teaming up of astrologer, client, and chart creates its own story and dynamics. This chapter examines that "something else" that arises when a chart jumps to life and shows how the astrologer's own participation in a reading can be crucial to its outcome. The astrologer must also know when to take up the role of either therapist or interpreter, while always staying tuned in to the symbolism of each unique chart, which is the lifeline to accurate and effective interpretation.

ASTROLOGY IN ACTION

CONDUCTING A READING

Only when the astrologer, client, and horoscope come together can astrological information then be translated into meaning. It is the astrologer's task to hold together all the threads of informing, illustrating, interpreting, and counseling as the reading unfolds.

When the astrologer turns consultant a whole new world opens up and there are all sorts of issues to consider and learn about, as discussed throughout this chapter. However, your first consideration is to have some kind of practical structure for a consultation, so where do you begin?

I always start a session by asking my client if he or she has ever had a chart done before and if so, when, was it interesting, helpful, and so on. I often start by talking about the Sun sign, too, as this is a good "warmer," being generally the only thing that someone may already know about his or her chart. Mostly people will tell you if they think they are typical of

their sign, or not, and this can be a helpful springboard into further conversation. I go on to explain that we will start with the general picture (the natal chart) and then look at what has been happening recently, what is happening now, and what will happen in the coming months (transits and progressions).

I move on by explaining that the Sun sign is just a small part of the horoscope and that the other planets can be just as important, often more so. When a client first stares at the jumble of hieroglyphics which is the chart, I usually say something reassuring like, "I know this looks complicated but it really isn't. These are

A successful reading is a dialogue, in which the client interacts with the reader.

just the glyphs, the shorthand that we use for the planets and signs. Here it is in English." I then give my client a sheet of paper that lists the signs of the ten planets and Ascendant. Hardly anyone ever looks at it again, but it takes the mystique out of the visual appearance of the chart, it gives the message that it is accessible, and it is also something for the client to take away.

START WITH THE PAST

I then spend no more than ten minutes on the natal chart, explaining key points in simple terms. How long you spend on the natal chart will vary from client to client, but I personally like to move on to timing measures fairly quickly, simply because these tend to bring the chart to life in a way that is meaningful for both the client and the astrologer. As already stated, it makes sense to work with some past transits and progressions first. This establishes the client's confidence in the astrology, and in you as the astrologer, and there is no more effective way of capturing someone's serious attention than demonstrating how the chart has already been accurate in terms of reflecting individual life changes or events. Similarly, working with past events first puts the astrologer on surer ground, as demonstrated in chapter six. It is like oiling the cogs of a sensitive machine and letting it warm up—only then can it run at full power and not break down on you.

Throughout a consultation I always have pen and paper to hand so that I can sketch the things I am saying. Visual communication can be very effective, such as simply drawing a circle with the horizontal line across it to show the Ascendant-Descendant when talking about relationships, or a planet on a dotted line to show a transit. Simple visuals of any kind will assist with the effort of listening and understanding.

LISTEN TO YOUR CHART

However, bear in mind that, even with the best will in the world, most people's concentration will start to waver after listening for more than about 15 minutes. Some astrologers like to start by doing most of the talking but, with the above in mind, I prefer to get the dialogue going as quickly as possible. In my view a successful consultation is always a conversation. If you are holding forth it is difficult for the client to speak out and interact with you, and you can then miss valuable pointers. This is because the client will always speak of what is in the chart, so your listening is just as important, if not more so, because only by listening closely to what the client says and how it is said can you locate the story astrologically. The client will nearly always guide you to what is important.

You may sometimes know in advance why a client wants to see you, but, more often than not, you won't know until you meet with him or her. The preparation work that you can do before the appointment—locating significance, identifying current transits and progressions—may give you a pointer or a good idea, but only the client will supply the true context, which is his or her own story. As already discussed, this is why jumping to conclusions or working with predetermined meanings is so risky and ineffectual.

· Where a reading goes after the first ten minutes or so is anybody's guess and your best preparation lies in your own receptivity. When a client comes to you for the first time you need to be prepared for anything to surface and to stay open to the symbolism so that you can locate in the chart what you are hearing.

Astrologers tend to "over prepare" because the thought of having nothing to say to the client, or running out of things to say, is scary. Drawing a total blank is the astrologer's nightmare, and this is why astrologers often shy away from client work, or will see a client only when armed with an artillery of paperwork. The fear of disappointing the client is ever present. Thankfully, in reality, this is an extremely rare occurrence for the astrologer who is technically surefooted and at home with planetary symbolism. However, in my own experience, and in that of colleagues too, it is also true to say that some charts work better than others. I have only ever had one chart in my entire practice that didn't work at all—the tale of which is recounted later in this chapter.

CASE STUDY — JANE AFFLICTED BY MARS AND URANUS

The importance of my own participation came home to me after a reading for a young woman some years ago, which I have always remembered vividly. She came to see me at home and although I did everything I could to try and put her at ease, she remained tense and tight-lipped. Any attempts to draw her into conversation were met with fierce resistance and all she said was, "I just want to know what my chart says. I just want to know what you see."

It is not unusual for clients to be reticent at first as many people have a fear of giving something away. They want you to see it first, so in this instance I dutifully went forward with the reading. But, with no interaction from her, I eventually talked myself to a standstill. This sense of being out on a limb was quite possibly how she experienced the world and was duly reflected in the chart. She had Libra rising with her chart ruler Venus detrimented in Aries, conjunct the Descendant, and unaspected by any other planet. I was also feeling the selfish aspect of this situation, symbolic of Venus in Aries (the ego and self) in total isolation except for its claim on the "the other" (conjunct Descendant), expressing itself in this woman demanding my efforts, yet refusing to corroborate or refute anything that I said. I did my best to draw out this symbolism with her but it brought no response.

Difficult task I moved away from Venus and persevered, knowing that it wasn't going to get any easier because the main feature of her chart was a difficult fixed T-square—a Mars/Uranus opposition (a volatile combination: anger, pain, rebellion, splitting off) both squaring into the Moon in Taurus in the eighth house (death, loss). With the Moon (mother, children) ruling the Midheaven (a parent), I thought this had to be something to do with her mother, the grimmest interpretation being that she was dead. I broached the subject of childhood and the role of her mother, drawing out the symbolism of the T-square, and explaining as I went along that we both needed to keep faith with what the chart was saying, as she had requested.

THE ASTROLOGER AS INTERPRETER

One of the hats that the astrologer must wear is that of interpreter. Careful listening means constantly converting the client's words into the language of astrological symbolism. Most of this conversion goes on in the astrologer's head and does not need to be spoken. Being a careful interpreter means that we must feel our way through each reading, picking up on what to translate and what to miss out, where we should expand and where we should abbreviate.

For this reason it is generally a mistake to start over-explaining the chart. The astrologer may be fascinated by a T-square or exalted Jupiter, but using this language to a client may generate the mystified question, "What does that mean?" It is then easy to get sidetracked into technical explanations, which mean little or nothing to your client, which is a waste of valuable time. In fact, most clients will not remember the sign of their Moon or Ascendant later as it does not have the same meaning for them as it does for the astrologer. Very few clients are interested in the astrology, they are more interested in what the astrologer has to say.

The most I got out of her was, "Mmm, maybe."

Concern about disappointing her started to dissipate in the face of my growing frustration. By this stage I was getting irritated and wondered if she always engendered this response in others who tried to get close to her, but she refused to talk about her relationships. I then decided to do something that I had never done before, or since, in a consultation. I decided that I would have one more try and that then I would tell her that I couldn't help her, and that she should keep her money and go and see someone else. In a last-ditch attempt to engage her I recapped in a firm voice about the Moon in her sign of exaltation yet in the house of loss and death, afflicted by Mars and Uranus, which to me spelled estrangement, anger, pain, or emotional trauma, that the "earth mother" qualities of the Taurus Moon had somehow been cut off from her, that maybe her childhood was not the idyllic image that she wanted it to be, and so on.

The whole story Maybe my silent decision communicated itself to her in some way, or maybe she realized that she was exhausting my patience and losing my interest. Whatever the reason, in the nick of time, she said, "As you have got so close I'll tell you everything." The key issue of the ensuing tale was that, as she put it, "I was given up for adoption." The moment I heard this I realized what had happened between us. With her Moon in Taurus almost exactly conjunct my own difficult Mars in Taurus she had angered me, and maybe had even triggered my feelings around the death of my own mother. I had risen to that anger in that I had decided to send her to another astrologer. Like the biological mother I, the astrological or symbolic mother, had nearly "given her up for adoption." We had come within a hair's breadth of reenacting the event that had caused her so much pain in her life. I was very relieved that we finally managed to communicate and were able to move on with the reading in a way that was mutually rewarding and therapeutic.

ASTROLOGY IN ACTION

THE ASTROLOGER AS THERAPIST

Any practicing astrologer will tell you that a consultation is not just about the horoscope as an objective exercise. The coming together of astrologer, client, and chart makes for a dynamic trio, pulling a reading very often into the world of therapy.

When I first started consulting, I quickly realized that clients were not coming just to find out their Moon sign or Ascendant. You will of course get clients who are genuinely interested in having their chart done, but nine times out of ten someone who seeks out an astrologer has a definite problem, question, or issue to resolve and is looking for answers that he or she has not been able to find elsewhere. This puts the astrologer in the rather delicate position of taking up the role of temporary therapist. The astrologer can learn a great deal from the principles of therapy, and I feel that some basic counseling skills are vital to an effective reading. For example, knowing where we

should sympathize or where we need to challenge, recognizing resistance or denial and knowing how to respond, or knowing when we should be quiet and let the client talk, can make a big difference to the success of a reading.

One of the main factors that distinguishes the astrologer from the therapist is time. In therapy there are repeat appointments, sometimes over a long period of time, during which the client will unravel his or her personal issues. With astrological work you may have a second or even third appointment, but there are a great deal of "one-off" consultations and the astrologer does not have the luxury of being able to return to a key point later. But the astrologer has something that the therapist doesn't—the horoscope. It is vital always to be guided by the chart, to grasp the astrological advantage of being able to zoom in on a symbol once you see it coming into play. In this way you are less likely to get sidetracked and the client is more likely to connect with what you have to say. A good way of practicing this skill is to do short readings, such as those offered at "psychic fairs." You will be amazed at what comes out when you only have half an hour.

SYMBOLIC TRICKERY

Realizing that conducting a reading is not just an objective exercise really comes home to the astrologer when the symbolism starts to become more apparent. The astrologer realizes that meaning and messages come to us in ways that cannot be explained just in terms of craft, and which can relate to the astrologer as well as the client. As astrologer Maggie Hyde explains, the objective language of astrology does not offer a rational explanation to phenomena that arise within the subjective world of symbolism:

"… these tricks of symbolism demand that the astrologer considers his or her participation in relation to the interpretation of the symbol.… The symbols not only reflect him or her but they do so in tricky, foxy, unconscious ways."

DRAWING A BLANK

The reading I referred to earlier—the chart that didn't work—turned out to be an example of this, although I didn't realize it at the time. A new client had made an appointment, we settled down to the consultation, and the nightmare happened—I drew a total blank. Absolutely nothing I said made any sense to my client. I battled on for a while but with my heart sinking, and in the end I was honest with her, and we abandoned the session. I was not a beginner when this happened, I just couldn't find a way into the chart.

NEPTUNE TRANSIT

I knew at the time that there was something else going on but hadn't got a clue as to what it might be. The only way I could explain this astrologically was that my client was a Pisces and in the middle of a long Neptune transit. I had attempted to draw out the Neptune symbolism but it hadn't rung any bells. For me, however, the experience was totally Neptunian—somehow I was the one who was totally at sea and trying to see through the fog. I wasn't struggling with any confusing issues at the time, so I didn't feel that it was a case of the client reflecting my own life back to me, which is a recognized phenomenon, as clients sometimes have an uncanny knack of presenting you with your own issues. If you are having trouble with work, you will have clients with work problems; if you are having a hard time with your partner, you will have clients with relationship problems; if you are feeling lonely, you will have clients who desperately want a relationship, and so on. This is what Jung termed the "secret mutual connivance" in therapeutic work, when other factors sneak in and symbolism plays tricks on

you, when the issue that should be the client's somehow becomes yours. So, it is quite possible that this client was telling me something about myself but, in typical Neptune fashion, I couldn't see what it was.

The other way of looking at any client situation is to remember that the consultation is very often a cameo of that person's life. If someone is friendly and easy to be with, then they are probably that way out in the world; if someone is cagey or suspicious, then this may reflect the way in which they approach life, and so on. With my Neptune client I wondered—too late—if this was a cameo of her life and was this the way that she made others feel, consciously or unconsciously? She sat serenely while I struggled to make her life take shape, feeling guilty when I couldn't deliver. This captured the archetypal Piscean struggle—how does the sign of mutable water take shape and form? One way is to pour itself into another or into someone else's mold, becoming the person that he or she imagines is desired. Even my feeling guilty added to this picture, as the sign of Pisces is associated with taking on the suffering of others. Looking back with hindsight, it is easy to see that her Piscean persona had somehow been projected on to me, but I wasn't quick enough to see it at the time.

MISSING THE POINT

The above story also speaks of how a rich symbolic experience can all too easily slip through the astrologer's fingers. The astrologer, dwelling on such experiences, may later make sense of what happened, but when the astrologer misses the point in the consultation, the client misses out.
It is often helpful, although not fail-safe, to keep hold of any ideas that take shape in your preparatory work. I remember drawing up a chart for a young man and noting that his Mercury was in detriment in Pisces, retrograde, and exactly square to my own Mercury. While I was working on his chart, Mercury was proving

to be important in the chart at a craft level, and I wondered if this man would lie to me, deliberately or by omitting details. When it came to the consultation I had forgotten this idea and it was only after it had ended that it came back to me.

As he left, I had the distinct impression that he wasn't satisfied, even though he had insisted that he was. The feeling that we hadn't talked about something important, quite probably a major issue, persisted and it was some time later that I discovered, by accident, that he was gay. Recalling some of our conversation it was, of course, then blindingly obvious. He had never used the word "her," only "that relationship" or "that person," he had not opened up about his love life, and had said several things that didn't seem to ring true. I had thought at the time that maybe he hadn't had any steady relationships and

was embarrassed by his lack of success. After some gentle but non-productive probing I had dropped the subject for fear of making him uncomfortable.

In this case, it was not surprising that I had felt that I had missed the point. As soon as I had mentioned women as opposed to neutral relationships, I had unwittingly backed this shy young man into a corner. This was a mortifying reminder for me never to be complacent or assume anything. Had I hung on to my original insight into the troubled Mercury, I may well have been both more challenging and more receptive.

VANESSA VENUS OF MOTHERHOOD

Last but by no means least comes a woman who was not a client but a friend. With such a fascinating tale to tell she willingly agreed to her horoscope being included in this book. When you first meet Vanessa she is everything you would expect from a Sun Leo, Sagittarius rising, with Mars in Sagittarius in the first house, ruled by an exalted Jupiter in the seventh house—warm, friendly, energetic, and kind.

The other planet in its sign of exaltation is the Moon (mother, babies, needs) in Taurus (earthy, fertile), conjunct the fifth-house cusp (children), sextile and dispositing the chart ruler Jupiter in Cancer (the sign of nurture and family). As you would expect this symbolizes a strong desire to have children—a desire that was frustrated for many years. Why?

Look again at her chart (see page 155) and you will see that the Moon is opposite Saturn in Scorpio, the sign that rules the reproductive system, and square to Pluto in the eighth—spelling absence or loss. In fact, this config-uration is just short of being a fixed T-square as the Saturn/Pluto square has a nine-degree orb, one degree over the orb allowed by strict craft rules. Similarly, the Sun in the

eighth house squares Saturn but the Sun square Moon has, again, a nine-degree orb. We may not end up with a bona fide T-square with either pattern but nevertheless both the lights (the life-givers) are afflicted—in stressful aspect—by the malefics, Saturn and Pluto.

Traumatic time Vanessa suffered the tragedy of two ectopic pregnancies. The first was in 1987 but she couldn't remember the date. I wondered whether it had been February, when the progressed Moon was conjunct Uranus (shocks, splits) in Cancer (children, the womb), very close to the eighth house, which is the domain of both death and surgery. The second was in February 1992 and there were no relevant progressions. But transiting Saturn was traveling from 9 to 12 degrees of Aquarius in that month, therefore picking out the natal Moon square Pluto, symbolizing both the loss of the baby and the surgery. Also, Jupiter was making its second, retrograde transit over Venus, who is ruler of the fifth house of children, and in its sign of fall, Virgo, a sign associated with infertility. Often the middle contact of a three-legged transit can be crucial, showing an unraveling of what has been achieved.

Over the next couple of years she and her husband decided to

invest in fertility treatment but every attempt failed. When Uranus started his transit opposite the eighth-house Sun in April 1995, coupled with a solar eclipse at 8.56 Taurus—conjunct her Moon—in the same month, the project was abandoned. Undeterred, Vanessa and her husband made the decision to adopt. This she recalled as being the middle of May, so I looked at the progressed chart for 15 May 1995. The progressed Sun on this day was at 9.30 Virgo and therefore applying by trine to her natal Moon at 9.34 Taurus.

A progression between the lights, and especially with the Moon on the fifth-house cusp, was

encouraging. But, no matter how wonderful the progression, nothing takes away the natal configuration—in this case the heavy duty Saturn and Pluto aspects—so they had an ordeal ahead of them, being subjected to a long vetting procedure by the adoption agency. Vanessa had lived abroad many times in her life—seen in Sagittarius rising; her chart ruler Jupiter exalted and in an angular house; the ruler of the Midheaven, Venus, conjunct the ninth-house cusp (all things foreign); and the Part of Fortune in the ninth—and had fond memories of her time in Hong Kong. They decided to adopt a Chinese baby.

Look again at Vanessa's chart and note the stunning symbolism for a decision to adopt a foreign, unwanted baby. Venus, often associated with motherhood and children, rules the fifth house of children, but is in fall and conjunct the ninth-house cusp (all things foreign). Venus also sextiles Vanessa's chart ruler Jupiter (the ruler of all foreign concerns) and Mercury (ruler of the seventh, and therefore showing Vanessa's husband) and trines the Moon on the fifth cusp. Mercury and Jupiter—rulers of the Ascendant and Descendant—conjunct in the seventh house of marriage and in the family sign of Cancer, both mediate the Moon-Venus trine.

New baby The happy ending to this story came in the middle of December 1996. On 10 December there was a new moon at 18.56 Sagittarius—conjunct Vanessa's Ascendant and her husband's Sun—and their new life as parents was about to begin. The green light came after Christmas, and on New Year's Day they flew to China. They checked into their hotel and waited. On the night of 5 January 1997 the hotel room phone rang with the news that their adopted daughter, Hannah, had arrived and please could they come down to the lobby to collect her. The formalities were over and Hannah was handed to them without further ado.

Here is the astrological picture on the day:

◆ The progressed Sun was at 9.30 Virgo, trine the Moon at the time the decision was made to adopt. At the time of adoption the progressed Sun was at 11.06 Virgo—applying to sextile Mercury in Cancer to within 8 minutes of arc. This seemed to be a fitting progression—the Sun lighting up the seventh-house Mercury (who rules all administration, form-filling, signatures, decisions, etc.), who mediates the Moon trine Venus, when the negotiations and paperwork are complete. The next solar progression would be the powerful progressed Sun conjunct the all-important Venus. This can also be said to be applying at this time as it would be exact just seven months later.

◆ Vanessa's progressed Ascendant was at 27.11 Capricorn, applying by square to the progressed Venus at 27.16 Libra. Remember that aspects in progressions are not as crucial as they are in the natal chart, so the square is not cause for concern. Here we simply see the Ascendant—the angle ruling Vanessa herself—coming together with Venus, ruler of the fifth house—her new daughter. Even transiting Venus on the day was at 24 degrees of Sagittarius—making her presence doubly felt by being conjunct Vanessa's first-house natal Mars at 25.50 Sagittarius.

◆ The progressed Moon was at 26.15 Scorpio, trine the progressed Uranus at 26.10 Cancer, which I thought spoke of the journey and the unusual "delivery" of their daughter.

◆ The progressed Moon was also catching up with the progressed Midheaven at 29.18 Scorpio.

With the angle of status and aspirations at 29 degrees—a critical degree—this was fitting symbolism for their new status of parenthood.

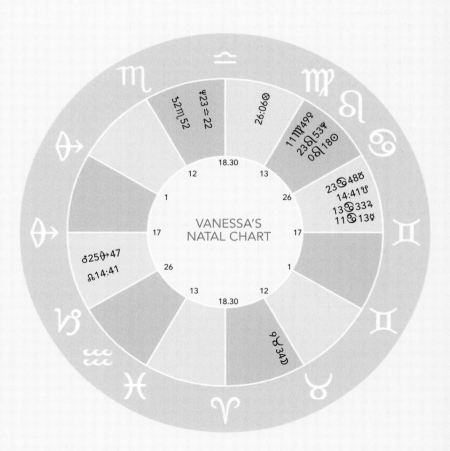

VANESSA'S NATAL CHART

155

This sample page from Aureas Editions' Complete Ephemerides 1920–2020 shows the planetary positions for January 2003.

GLOSSARY

ACD Adjusted Calculation Date

Air signs Gemini, Libra, and Aquarius

Angles Beginning of houses 1,4,7, and 10, respectively the Ascendant, I.C., Descendant, and Midheaven

Angle marking Beginning of the first house

Angular houses Houses 1,4,7, and 10

Angular planets Planets conjunct the angles or in the angular houses

Applying—or perfecting Two planets moving together by progression to form an aspect

Ascendant—or rising sign Sign rising over the eastern horizon at the time of birth.

Aspect The nature of the distance between two planets

Aspectarian Tables in the ephemerides that list the type and time of daily aspects

Cadent houses Houses 3,6,9, and 12

Cardinal signs Aries, Cancer, Libra, and Capricorn

Chart ruler The planet ruling the sign on the Ascendant

Conjunction Two planets less than eight degrees apart

Cusp The dividing line between two houses

Cusp—born "on the cusp" Someone born within a day of the Sun changing sign

Cycle Time a planet takes to make a full orbit of the zodiac

Daily motion How far a planet moves in 24 hours

Descendant Angle marking beginning of the seventh house of partnership

Detriment Planet in the sign opposite its sign of dignity

Dignity—or rulership Planet in its own sign

Dispositor A planet disposits another planet if it is in the other planet's own sign

Dissociate A blind aspect

Earth signs Taurus, Virgo, and Capricorn

Elements Fire, earth, air, and water

Ephemerides Tables listing the daily motions of planets

Exaltation Planet in its strongest sign

Fall Planet in the sign opposite its sign of exaltation

Fire signs Aries, Leo, and Sagittarius

Fixed signs Taurus, Leo, Scorpio, and Aquarius

Fixed stars Slow-moving stars that appear to be stationary

Grand Cross Aspect pattern of four planets, each 90 degrees apart

Grand Trine Aspect pattern of three planets, each 120 degrees apart

House ruler The planet that rules the sign on the cusp of the house

House tables Tables listing the sign and degree on each house cusp for any latitude

Houses Division of the horoscope into 12 segments

I.C. (Imum Coeli) Angle marking beginning of the fourth house

Ingress Time when a planet moves into the next sign

Inner house cusps Divisions of the horoscope marking the beginning of houses 2,3,5,6,8,9,11, and 12

Kite Aspect pattern formed by a grand trine with one of the three planets in opposition to a fourth

Lights—or luminaries The Sun and the Moon

Lunar eclipse When the Moon is obscured by the shadow of the Earth at the time of a full Moon

Lunations New or full Moons

Midheaven—or M.C. (Medium Coeli) Angle marking beginning of the tenth house

Minute of arc One-sixtieth of a degree

Mixed reception Two planets, one in the other's sign of dignity, one in the other's sign of exaltation

Mode Cardinal, fixed, or mutable element

Moon's nodes Imaginary points at which the Moon cuts across the ecliptic

Mutable signs Gemini, Virgo, Sagittarius, and Pisces

Mutual reception Two planets that are in each other's signs of dignity

Natal planets Position of the planets in the birth chart

Native The person to whom the chart belongs

Nativity The birth chart or horoscope of an individual

Natural house A planet in its own house of rulership

Opposition Two planets 180 degrees apart

Orb The number of degrees either side of an exact position for an aspect still to be allowed

Part of Fortune A fortunate degree of the chart, derived from the formula of the Ascendant, plus the Moon, minus the Sun

Partile An aspect that is exact by degree and minute

Perfecting see "Applying"

Progressed to natal Aspects made by progressed planets or angles to planets or angles in the natal chart

Progressed to progressed Aspects made between progressed planets

Progression A symbolic timing measure for moving the planets on year by year

Quadruplicity Signs of the same mode

Quinqunx—or inconjunct Two planets 150 degrees apart

Retrograde planet Planet apparently moving backward

Returns When a planet completes its orbit, returning to its original position at the time of birth

Rising sign see "Ascendant"

Rulership see "Dignity"

Semi-sextile Two planets 30 degrees apart

Semi-square Two planets 45 degrees apart

Separating Two planets moving apart after having been in exact aspect

Sesquiquadrate Two planets 135 degrees apart

Sextile Two planets 60 degrees apart

Solar eclipse When the Sun is obscured by the shadow of the Moon at the time of a new Moon

Square Two planets 90 degrees apart

Star of David Aspect pattern formed by six planets, all sextile to each other

Stationary planet A planet turning retrograde or direct

Stellium Four or more planets conjunct in same sign

Succeedent houses Houses 2,5,8, and 11

Synastry Compatibility revealed by comparing two horoscopes

Timing measures Transits and progressions

Transit An orbiting planet in aspect to a natal planet

Trine Two planets 120 degrees apart

Triplicity Signs of the same element

T-square An aspect pattern formed by two planets in opposition, both in square to a third

Water signs Cancer, Scorpio, and Pisces

Yod—or finger of fate Aspect pattern formed by two planets in sextile, both quinqunx to a third planet

ACKNOWLEDGMENTS

I would particularly like to thank friends and fellow astrologers Mike Edwards and Sally Kirkman as the two people I pestered most for information. Thank you for your patience, positive support, and willingness to help out at the drop of an email.

To everyone at the Company of Astrologers, especially Geoffrey Cornelius and Maggie Hyde from whom I have learned so much over the years. Thanks especially, Maggie, for your insightful editing of Ruth's story. A special mention to the late Derek Appleby, who was simply a fountain of knowledge and inspiration at a crucial time.

Thank you to *Zest* magazine astrologer Louise Ronane, Carole West at the Astrological Lodge of London, and Diana McMahon-Collis of TABI, again for willingness to help out with varying requests.

A big thank you to my treasured twin sister Sue, who enthusiastically read the manuscript from beginning to end, and who was an unflagging source of belief, ideas, and encouragement throughout.

To my agent, the very special Annie Tatham-Mannall, who gently kept me on track by always saying exactly the right thing at exactly the right time.

To friend and therapist Paul Hitchings for all your input over the years, so much of which has worked its way into this material.

To Maggie Bosman for friendship and loving care that is so deeply valued and appreciated, even when I take you for granted!

Grateful thanks to all my clients who allowed their readings to be used.

To the team at Carroll and Brown for your collective expertise, especially managing editor Michelle Bernard, who was thrown in at the astrological deep end and swam.

Last, but never least, to my "earth partner" Charles ♥, to whom this book is dedicated.

Carroll & Brown would also like to thank: Aureas Editions, www.aureas.com, for granting permission for us to reproduce part of *The Complete Ephemerides 1920–2020*

W. Foulsham for granting permission to reproduce part of *Raphael's Ephemeris 2004*

Additional design and editorial assistance Emily Cook, Stuart Moorhouse
Production Director Karol Davies
Production Controller Nigel Reed
Computer Management Paul Stradling and Nicky Rein
Picture Researcher Sandra Schneider
Indexer Madeline Weston

PICTURE CREDITS